CW00674509

FROM NOW ON—EVERY SEX ACT OF SEX MAGICK!

So says the author to those who ~~have~~ ......
tice of Sex Magick. The ritual is easy; the attitude natural; the energy created the most potent of all energies to come from within man.

Based on the teachings given forth in the secret order G∴B∴G∴, the author details the means for reaching the height of physical and spiritual ecstasy. The magickal imagination transforms the individual personality into a manifested form of the Divine Lover, the Higher Self, the Holy Guardian Angel, C.G. Jung's Daemon.

Through Sex Magick one realizes the great power of sex-created energy. It "spills out" as other magical powers— those not intentionally invoked but magically useful. Mr. Culling gives methods for obtaining or strengthening specific abilities or attitudes and thereby receiving the appropriate inspiration. This is not the "magic of sex"; Sex Magick is using sex as a potent vehicle for magical attainment. And it works!

Author of:
    The Incredible I Ching
    The L.R.I. I Ching
    The Complete Magick Curriculum of the
        Secret Order G∴B∴G∴

For I am divided for love's sake,
for the chance of union.

The Book of the Law
Chapter 1:29

Sex Magick

Louis T. Culling

1988
Llewellyn Publications
St. Paul, Minnesota 55164-0383, U.S.A.

International Standard Book Number: 0-87542-110-5
Library of Congress Catalog Number: 85-45955

First Edition, 1971
First Printing, 1971
Second Printing, 1986
Third Printing, 1986
Fourth Printing, 1988

Library of Congress Cataloging-in-Publication Data
Culling, Louis T.
  Sex magic.

  Rev. ed. of: A manual of sex magick. 1st ed. 1971.
  1. Sex.   2. Occult sciences.   I. Culling, Louis T.
Manual of sex magick.   II. Title.
HQ64.C86   133.4'3   85-45955
ISBN 0-87542-110-5

Cover Painting: John Waltrip

Produced by Llewellyn Publications
Typography and Art property of Chester-Kent, Inc.

Published by
LLEWELLYN PUBLICATIONS
A Division of Chester-Kent, Inc.
P.O. Box 64383
St. Paul, MN 55164-0383, U.S.A.

Printed in the United States of America

APOLOGIA

There are those who will find this manual to be insufficiently titillating or pornographic, while on the other hand, there will be those for whom the sexual content is out of bounds for what they falsely regard as normal and moral. It is regrettable that there can be no happy medium which will satisfy both sides: unfortunately, this is impossible.

There will be others who are astute enough to treasure this manual as a real rariora of authentic Sex Magick, but they will not perform the practices as given herein: for this, it is regrettable also.

It is to those who will be inspired to follow out the practices that I fondly address this work. It is sufficient that they aspire to self-transcendence. They need no seven year itch of the intellect to stimulate the mind, to discover why and how Sex Magick works. It is the result of sincere and regular practice that counts.

In stating that the real secrets of the contents of this manual have been closely guarded for many centuries and that this is the first time they have been revealed in print, admittedly poses two question.

(1) Why are they now being revealed?

(2) How does it happen that the author breaks the oath of secrecy and reveals all?

The answer is that the highly secret order to which I

belonged decided that the time was rapidly approaching when such secrecy would not be mandatory and that it could be openly revealed ten years after the order closed its doors for all time. I was chosen to do so, but only under two conditions.

(1) If and when I would be ready to assume "full responsibility, magickally".

(2) That it be given forth in the right manner and under the proper conditions.

This book is the result, adhering to those conditions.

FOREWORD

For ten years I have been acquainted with the author of this manual and with his preoccupations contained in this book.

I would like to contribute my share in helping to clarify various points. Involved are such things as "erotogenesis of religion," the specialty of psychiatrist Theodore Schroeder. *Genesis* means 'to create'. Merely because a strong sex force and drive can be responsible for increasing religious emotion even far beyond the normal, it does not give evidence that sex creates religion: this is an unforgivable *non sequitur.*

On the other hand, we must admit, yea insist, that many of our propensities are greatly increased by a strong sex force. I am reminded of the occasion of taking a woman singer to a singing teacher specializing in classical concert singing. After he had tested her voice, he said to me, "She has a nice voice but not to make a real singer. Neither I nor any other teacher can make a real singer of her, because she has no ovaries." (Meaning small sex force.) Even literally he was correct: her ovaries had been removed ten years earlier.

Real love depends also upon a strong sex force to produce that deep abiding love that is beyond intellectual analysis. Thinking that a sexual affair is the same as a love affair is a tricky trap to fall into. Love may be involved in a sexual congrex but love and sex are two separate things. Here is the tremendous, continuous circle of incredible force. The sexual union can increase the love between two people, and, on the other hand, love can intensify sex, with more sex increasing love, and so on.

Alas, if they are not holding, at least unconsciously, to some of the principles of sex as outlined herein, there can come a surfeit of sex play, and antagonism will gradually replace love in this self-winding circle. Let this book put you on guard.

Clarke A. Walker
Educator in Psychology

CONTENTS

A Brief History of Western Magick   *1*

Introduction to the Three Degrees of Sex Magick   *5*

Alphaism: The First Degree   *17*

Dianism: The Second Degree   *21*

Dianism: Elaborated   *39*

Quodosch: The Third Degree   *51*

The Magickal Child   *71*

Appendices

Appendix I
     Damiana: The Psychic Aphrodisiac   *94*

Appendix II
     Marijuana and Champagne   *99*

Appendix III
     Sufi Philosophy   *102*

Appendix IV
     The Yi King and Sex Magick   *131*

ILLUSTRATIONS

The Templar Cross   *facing page 1*

Lust   *facing page 21*

The Star   *facing page 51*

The Sigil of Baphomet   *facing page 128*

The Cauldron   *facing page 131*

Yi King Hour Table   *following page 133*

The 64 Hexagrams   *facing page 137*

An ancient cross of the crusading Order of Templars.

A BRIEF HISTORY OF WESTERN MAGICK

There are many who insist upon evaluating various magick practices and philosophy by such things as its antiquity. Therefore, a brief history of Western Sex Magick, which has been practiced by high initiates for a known period of one thousand years to this present day, is well advised.

There are those who stoutly maintain that all Occultism and Magick originated in the Far East. Even though this may be so in going back to unrecorded history, nevertheless, for many centuries there have been essential differences between the East and the West.

Again, there are those who maintain that there is nothing in Western Magick that is not in the Eastern. Their arguments are astute enough but there is one flaw—they do not know enough Western Magick to know about the very essential differences.

It is hazardous to go back beyond the Middle Ages for documented history of Magick in Europe, dating the Middle Ages from 400 A.D. to 1541 A.D. The earlier part of this is what is called the Dark Ages, with Europe losing most of its culture to such a great extent that the Semites (Arabs and Jews) put Europe back on its feet, so to speak.

For clarity and convenience we date this new emergence of Europe at the time of the Crusades, from the eleventh century to the fourteenth century, inclusive.

Among the various knighthood orders of the Crusades,

the one of importance to us is the Order of Knights Templars, established in Jerusalem in 1118, for the protection of pilgrims on their way to the Holy Sepulcher.

Contrary to popular notion, the only time of outright war during the Crusades was in the time of Saladin (1174-1193), Sultan of Syria, who determinedly fought the Crusaders. Even in his time there were periods of truce with one order—the more civilized Knights Templar Order—and at times there was even fraternizing with the enemy Arabs. Many of the Templars of higher rank were initiated in the then very secret Arabian Order, the Sufis. They thus became initiated members of the sanctum of Sex Magick. Here is the beginning of real Western Sex Magick. From the days of the crusading Templars to this day, these secrets have been kept inviolate, even though the Church Inquisition and the State persecuted the Templars to the point near complete extinction.

The Holy Roman Christian Church had instigated an unchristian war against the Arabs of Jerusalem, unless it is considered Christian when in the "First Crusade," on Friday, July 15, 1099, thirty thousand Moslems were massacred in Jerusalem before the blood lust was satiated. It is deemed necessary to recount this unsavory mess in order to explain various incidents between the Church and one of the crusading orders, the Order of Knights Templars.

After the Crusades, the Templars in France became the richest and most powerful international banking establishment of the Middle Ages. But their doom was sealed.

King Phillipe le Be?coveted their wealth. Pope Clement was easily persuaded to cooperate by sanctioning a charge against the Templars for heresy, sacrilege, blasphemy, and sexual perversion. On Friday, October 13, 1307, King Phillipe issued the orders for the arrest of all known

Templars. These were turned over to the Inquisitors of the Holy Roman Apostalic Catholic Church for interrogation by the Grand Inquisitor General of France. Anyone who knows anything about the ways of the Inquisition certainly need not be surprised to read that soon fifteen thousand Templars were either unmercifully tortured, starved to death, or burned at the stake.

Grand Master Jaques de Molay was one of several thousand who got the most merciful treatment—burning at the stake. Then came what I call a good example of "valueless compensation". De Molay had said, "I cite you two before the Tribunal of God." Within one month, Pope Clement died in torment with the dread disease *Lupus*. Within eight months, King Phillipe was killed in a hunting accident. However, this may well have been a tremendous, persisting inspiration to the few remaining Knights Templars who turned to secrecy and took their movement underground.

Although the persecuting Inquisitors may have tortured some of the Templars into telling about the Sufi secrets of Sex Magick, nevertheless all of this meant only "sex perversion" to the Inquisitors. To this day it is the same. Although the ideals and practices of Sex Magick are far more idealistic and spiritually inspiring than the ways of common sexual relations, it is not an uncommon thing for restricted minds to yelp, "Sex Magick! That's immoral sex perversion!"

The Sufi secret workings did not die with the end of the Templars. They were perpetuated through descending generations of apparently unorganized individuals. The chain is evidenced in the writings of such isolated individuals as Levi, Papus, Franz Hartmann, Hargrave Jennings, Edward Kelley, Thomas Vaughn and others, who revealed in their writings that they were guardians of the secrets, but the actual secrets were not set in writing.

(There was one woman, Ida Craddock, who actually did put out a few of the secrets in a privately circulated manuscript. For this, she was unmercifully persecuted by acquaintances and even by friends.)

The first record of any organized group was one of an obscure society in Austria and Germany at the early turn of this century. This was transmitted to England under the name of O∴T∴O∴, Order of Oriental Templars, headed by Aleister Crowley, which was in turn transmitted to the Order G∴B∴G∴, 1932, which closed its doors in 1937.

The secret workings of the Sufis were also given to Europe in another way, through Alchemy, from the Arabic *Al-kimiya,* which originated in Arabia but had made strides in Europe as early as the noted Swiss philosopher, physician, and alchemist, Paracelsus (1493-1541). There are four kinds of alchemical writings: (1) medicinal, (2) actual chemical and metallic experiments, (3) mystical philosophy, (4) disguised Sex Magick. In the writings of the alchemists there are scores of disguised writings on Sex Magick, but one must be well acquainted with the subject in order to decode these writings.

It is found that many of the terms used in these writings are uniquely valuable to employ; therefore, at the end of this text, there are listed a number of key words used in the alchemical writings. In fact, these words were originally exclusive keys of Sex Magick which the writers inserted in the metallic and chemical format of Alchemy.

This sums up the relevant history of Western Sex Magick which did not come from the Far East, but from Arabia and is distinctly and uniquely Western, both in its religious philosophy and in its workings.

INTRODUCTION TO THE THREE DEGREES
OF SEX MAGICK

Unprejudiced and informed people are not inclined to deny the physiological activity of what specialists call "erotogenesis of love and religion". It seems silly to deny the operation of what is called a *mechanism*, but this is not to say that love and religion do not have their own prior existence in the psyche. Such psychiatrists as Reich and Jung treat this existence very extensively.

For one year I have been racking my brain for a good exemplar in which there exists two individuals involved in both erotogenic love and a very real love that transcends sexually generated love. I have found one, but it is first necessary to give some preliminary explanations.

There was an aging doctor living in Pennsylvania who felt very deeply about the impending extinction of the Great Gray Wolf of the North-west. He decided to have a wolf refuge on his farm. Indeed, the lobo is no longer numerous and it was only after much time and expense that he had a colony of a dozen wolves. The wolves were not closely confined; they were in a large fenced area.

The nature of the lobo is very basic. One outstanding characteristic is that they are very selective in choosing a mate. To resort to a common expression, they must fall in love, perforce erotogenic love, because it is between two of the opposite sex. And they mate for life.

When the doctor saw that two of his wolves had

accepted each other as mates and had mated, he put them in an enclosure separate from the other wolves.

Getting enough to eat is a lifelong problem of the wolf. When wolves see an animal that has fallen to the ground or is crippled, the immediate instinct to kill for food is overpowering even if the belly is full. This drive is so powerful that the wolf is not deterred by any other thing.

Now it so happened that the good doctor and the male wolf were in great mutual affection—that kind of love which I have both known and seen between a man and a dog, where the dog seems to regard the man as God and the man regards the dog as a gift from God. This love can be as deep as the love between two human beings and any person who says it cannot be, is a mile from knowing what he is talking about. The doctor had not achieved the same rapport with the female wolf; she remained skittish and aloof.

The doctor and his wolves had gained wide publicity and there had been an extensive account about him in *Life* magazine, in which he tells the following story.

While he was in the enclosure of the two mated wolves, he stumbled and fell prostrate to the ground. On one side he saw the female crouched, ready for the spring, and he thought, "Is this going to be the end of me?" On the other side he saw the male, already leaping and in the air. Then he said to himself, "My God! This is my death for certain." But the male had leaped over the doctor and had thrown its full 150 pounds onto its mate, and had knocked it prostrate.

This is the exemplar where it is shown that real love far transcends mere sexual love. (Remember, wolves mate for life.)

In living Nature there is a sentience of something that is superior to one's self, with Man and many other living things. This is the basis upon which the religious feeling rests. There are concomitants, or so it appears, of love, aspiration, inspiration, veneration, an abiding desire to be closer to anything that brings the feeling of the Divine Spirit, and even such as the pure joy of existence. (It may not be intelligent to denegrade *appearances.* The appearance that the sun rises every morning contains a great bit of reality, while the astronomical fact that the daily axial rotation of the earth brings us in line with the sun's rays bears no significance to animals or to more than one-half the population of this earth.)

Indeed, when we get into abstractions, replete with unknowns, the appearance is the basis for the scientific theory or determination.

After this digression, we come to a subject that runs throughout this book. To use a term from psychology, it is called a *complex,* which briefly defined, is a system of ideas and/or memories which, in a disguised form, exerts a dominant influence upon the personality, even to the point of being autonomous in action. To expand on this, a complex is born when a person has an idea or ideas and particularly feelings and emotions of a strong, intense nature, which are strengthened by many repetitions of the same until finally this force becomes autonomous i.e., the force persists without any willed intention of the subject.

However, the above definition describes cases that are more or less of a psychopathic nature, in which the person is a victim of a non-self-willed idea which manifests in a disguised form. In these cases the complex does not always break out until many years later. It is always, from the beginning to the end, a non-self-directed and unwilled force.

But there is another kind of complex in which the person gains, instead of becoming the victim, and it does not manifest in a disguised form, albeit this complex is also autonomous. We are concerned in Magick with the willed, intentional, and self-directed complex which we call the *Bud-Will*, or the *Magickal Offspring*. Its genesis is self-willed and self-directed and of a definitely desired nature. A tremendous emotional and willed force is necessary for this genesis, and also a great magickal imagination. There is only one known method for creating the magickal Bud-Will, which is the method of Western Sex Magick, as given forth in this book.

Occasionally the Bud-Will is generated without this method, as shown in the following example where Fritz Kreisler played the violin for me.

The setting was a theatre in Sedalia, Missouri, where I was the relief pipe organist with the orchestra. The scheduled attraction for that night was the appearance of the incomparable violinist Fritz Kreisler. In the late afternoon when the theatre was dark, I went back stage to get some music from my storage place. There I was struck nearly speechless to see Kreisler himself. It turned out that he, like myself, was deeply interested in mysticism and we fell into a wonderful conversation.

Then his eye fell upon the violin belonging to the orchestra leader. He opened the case and plucked a few notes and said, "Not a bad fiddle. What shall I play for you?" I told him that I had never achieved any real empathy with the spirit of Hungarian Gypsy music and would like to hear something of that nature. "Ah," he said. "Then I shall not play any written music for you. I am going to improvise."

He went all out playing Gypsy music, but I was so enchanted with watching and listening to the music of my idolized Fritz Kreisler that I was not conscious of having attained any better appreciation of such music, though later events showed that I had unconsciously attained to the object of my desire.

I had twelve compositions by Kreisler and during the ensuing twelve show-days I played all of them. Then I was informed that the organist at the opposition house was leaving. I wanted the place at that theatre very much and hurried over to have a talk with the owner.

He led me to the organ console and said, "I am a Hungarian. Play some Gypsy music for me."

I knew only a few simple songs. What should I do? With small confidence I began to improvise. (A well-tutored musician knows that the Gypsy scale has, in distinction from our standard scale, a flat third, a sharp fourth, and a flat sixth.)

Suddenly I was startled and enchanted by my own music. It was evident that it was getting to the owner too. When I had finished there were tears in his eyes and his voice quavered as he said, "You win, hands down."

It had been a complex—autonomous. Great strength had been given to the complex by the quotidian mechanism i.e., playing Kreisler music everyday for two weeks, which is more than mere mnemonics. His music was what is called the *magickal link.*

The reader will note that this operation was not initiated by repressed desires but rather by willed intent, fortified by aspiration and inspiration. (No matter how great the results of man's desires might be, only too frequently "spin-offs" of the results can be very undesirable. This point is treated later in this book.)

The Kreisler exemplar contains no sex magick technic; this has been intentionally so selected. Again take note that Kreisler's playing for me created a tremendous emotional and inspirational force in me, and also created the energized and magickal imagination, and that this force was kept alive and enhanced by repetition i.e., by playing his compositions everyday.

Rarely does one's emotion and imagination, plus repetition, enchant one to such intense inspiration, but this was fortified by a concomitant desire and aspiration. But take note in this text how and why, in sex magick congrex, this great fire of the magickal imagination is generated and fed.

But when one wants to create the autonomous Bud-Will without any aid or method, it is next to impossible to invoke the required *energized enthusiasm* of the magickal imagination. But there is a method, a supermethod, which is Sex Magick. So potent is Sex Magick that even when practiced half-heartedly or by the inept, there is always some result.

Let all be forewarned. There is some psychological, or magickal, result in just plain physical intercourse wherein there is neither inspiration nor aspiration. The result is deadening to all the finer sensibilities, and the man and his wife lose what mutual affection that they may have had. And if they do not seek a separation it is merely because they are in the rut of a habit pattern.

Another type of exemplar should now be given. Erotogenesis of religion, sex, love, aspiration, and Magick are often, even typically, involved in the same complex and are almost inseparable. This is the point of the following story of intended and willed Sex Magick.

The subject of this example was a member of the secret section of the Order of Sufis of Arabia and Persia. I was a member of the Order of Palladians, which by devious routes, possessed the secrets of the Sufis. It was due to this quasi-fraternal bond that George X told me about his experience in a town in southern Missouri as follows.

It was there that I met a preacher from one of those nondenominational churches. He told me that within three weeks the annual baptismal would be held at the creek near town.

"It's not like it used to be," he said. "I used to have that creek working alive with them, but I don't have the spirit any more."

I told him that I was an ordained minister and would help him put some real fire into it. He was overjoyed at the idea and he invited me to have supper at his house.

I met his wife there, and the aura of her sex pulsed out a yard from her body. For religious energized enthusiasm and force she had it, but the years had taken that "it" away from him. I gave him the job of starting immediately to recruit a number of men to prepare for a big barbecue at the creek and told his wife to come to my room on the following day to get an outline for her part.

In my room, she started right out saying that she felt that I really had something, and she would do anything to help put it over—anything. I told her that I intended to use certain secret, powerful, magick technics, and reassured her that anything directed toward religious ends could not possibly be black Magick.

Then I came right out with it and said, "I want you to sacrifice yourself on the altar of love for sake of union with the Divine Spirit."

Well, from that day, and for almost every night for three weeks, we made magick. (From the Persian poets comes the spiritual part, and from the *Arabian Nights* the sensual.)

I then thumbed through a copy of the *Arabian Nights* and read: "She thrust her tongue in his mouth like a tit-bit and the hour was such that maketh a man to forget. She girded him with her legs whereupon he made themselves proof amain as he cried out, 'O sire of the Chin—veils twain' and he breached the citadel in its four corners. So there befell the mystery concerning which there is no inquiry. There is no majesty and there is no might save in Allah, the Glorious and the Great."

Well, that Sex Magick, which you call the Bud-Will, worked greater than my fondest hopes. She and I both were like John the Baptist—the spirit was with us. We inspired over a hundred to be submerged in the waters of redemption. Persistently autonomous it was, even in an unexpected way. In my business I found myself turning on the religious charm and my sales were greatly increased for a long time.

The actual technic of the Sex Magick involved in this exemplar is explained in a later chapter. Here the man and the woman had attained to a condition, transcending the normal self, of "getting the spirit," of being inspired baptisers. Now then, how was this accomplished?

George X had been practicing what he knew of Sufi Sex Magick. Magick with *intent* (sometimes without apparent intent and often subversive) is the first step. This intent must be followed by *aspiration,* and the aspiration must be fortified with the *imagination.* It is not far amiss to state that the magickal imagination is 75 per cent of all willed Magick.

Psychologists recognize that imagination can be as real as anything else, but it is *subjective reality* that is meant. To be efficient in operative Magick, powerful and realistic imagination is necessary. The imagination must be energized and intense enough to produce a vital subjective reality.

George X and his instructed partner, were, with will, directing the imagination that they were inspired baptisers.

During the sexual congrex, the physical and emotional ecstasy is to be welcomed, but it is then, in turn, directed to feed the fire of the imagination, which is always kept in mind. Sexual ecstasy, instead of being indulged in per se, is directed to fire the imagination of the objective and is the most potent Magick.

Although Sex Magick can be used for the attainment of materialistic objectives, nevertheless there should be a high veneration for the whole operation.

Regardless of all peripheral objectives, the abiding central aim should be the *attainment of the knowledge and conversation of the Holy Guardian Angel,* or the *Daemon* as Jung calls it, or by many another name throughout time.

This central aim should always be an attitude in the operation. For this, the general technic is to forget the personality of the partner is congrex and to imagine and visualize her or him as a touchable manifestation of one's own Divine Lover, the Daemon. To actually experience this leaves one a bit lost for words. I have resorted therefore to the use of some poetry, a portion of Aleister Crowley's poem "Divine Synthesis". The man, trancelike, imagines that he has reached the impending end of his years. In the poem he stands high on a mountain peak and he looks down upon the valley which holds his memories of the past. What he says about the many women he has known in sexual congrex is a poetic way of describing the above referenced attitude, of visualizing the partner as a visible manifestation of God, the Divine Daemon, the Heavenly Lover, and the magickal results therefrom.

Prosper chance, this poetry tells more than would my own inadequate words.

Divine Synthesis

When I think of the many women I have loved from
    time to time,
White breasts and living bosoms where a kiss might
    creep or climb,
As on a mountain summit in the thunders and the
    snow,
I look to the shimmering valley and weep: I loved
    you so!
You were many indeed, but your love for me was
    one.
Then I perceived the stars to reflect a single sun.
Not burning suns themselves, in furious regular race,
But mirrors of midnight, lit to remind us of His Face.
Then I beheld the truth: ye are stars that give me
    light;
But I read you aright and learn I am walking in the
    night.
I saw the breaking light, and the clouds fled far away:
It was the resurrection of the Golden Star of Day.
And now I live in Him: my heart may trace the years
In drops of virginal blood and springs of virginal tears.
I love you now again with an undivided song.
I saw in your dying embraces the birth of a new
    embrace:
In the tears of your pitiful faces, another Holier Face.
Unknowing it, undesiring, your lips have led me
    higher;
You have taught me purer songs beyond your souls'
    desire;
You have taught me midnight vigils, when you smiled
    in amorous sleep:
You have even taught me a woman's way to weep.
So, even as you helped me, blindly without your will,

*So shall the Angel faces watch for your own souls
    still.*
A little pain and pleasure, a little touch of time,
*And you shall blindly reach to the glorious and
    sublime;*
*You shall gather up your girdles to make ready for
    the way,*
*And by the Cross of Suffering climb seeing to the
    Day.*
*Then we shall meet again in the Presence of the
    Throne,*
*Not knowing; yet in Him!—Oh Thou! knowing as we
    are known.*

ALPHAISM: THE FIRST DEGREE

Alphaism refers to the first letter of the greek alphabet, Alpha, the foundation and the beginning. Alphaism would not even be classified as a degree except for the fact that the results achieved by this discipline are very necessary to serve as an aid in the technic of the remaining two degrees.

Magickal chastity is the objective of the First Degree. This does not imply long periods of sexual abstinence. Despite the propaganda concerning the great spiritual attainment resulting from sexual continence, there has been no credible evidence that long celibacy has produced any beneficial results of any kind, among normal, average, western people. What it might do for the Far Eastern races is another matter and is also questionable.

Where there is no sexual outlet of any kind (including emotions and desires), then because there is no demand made upon the production of gonads the organs become gradually weaker in this activity. If this extends over a long period of time, the sex force is decreased to a minimum. The one exception to this is where there has been a sexual leakage during the period of celibacy and the production of gonads continues in order to compensate for the loss.

We resort to the testimony of the greatest master of transcendental Magick, Aleister Crowley. He took nothing for granted. He vowed to do everything that was traditionally against the rules of Magick and to do next to nothing where it said to be a must. During an extended practice of magickal chastity for four months, he testified that both his intellectual and inspirational writings had not been increased in quantity or quality. On the other hand, he said that during a period of orgiastic sex for four months, his writings had not been decreased in quantity or quality. So much for any supposed benefits for a period of four months. Others have given like testimony for periods lasting five years.

Then also, Max Heindel of the Rosicrucian Fellowship, whose religion embraced a disdain of sex relations as a means of pleasure, wrote: "One may practice celibacy and the 'spinal spirit fire' may flow to the crack of doom, but still not awaken the spiritual center."

Alpha chastity as a practicing magickal discipline is quite another thing. Magickal chastity does not forbid sexual union for pleasure and joy: it simply demands that it also be a dedicated sex magick rite, which is real magickal chastity.

Magickal chastity is a practice where the magician has no emotions about sex between the occasions of sexual congrex. He (and his partner, if possible) do not allow the mind or feelings to dwell upon sex at any time between their congrex magick practices. Particularly, the imagination must not be allowed to have fantasies upon the subject. Thus, when the night time for the congrex comes, they have not blown off steam during the day. More important, the imagination has not been stultified by erotic pictures. If during the days between the sexual congrex the person allows himself to be titillated physically, mentally, erotically, or emotionally, and with stimulated imagination, then at the actual congrex one of two things will happen. The past erotic imagination, having stimulated a strong erotic drive, will leave no room for the magickal imagination; or the erotic imagination of the preceding days will have drained, as it were, the ability to generate the magickal imagination during the sexual congrex. The imagination is not to be used until the practice of the Second Degree, and then it should bloom forth with all the ecstatic imagination possible.

In the heat of the beginning enthusiasm, the magickal partners may be practicing the Second Degree every night; we therefore see that the period of Alphaism is only the daytime between nights. However, let it not be forgotten that the practice of Alphaism is a must for one's remaining sexual life if continuing with the other two degrees, and we assume that if a person once begins these degrees, he stops only because of old-age incapacity.

From now on, every sexual union is to be an act of Sex Magick, and the intervening periods are to be for building up all of one's forces, as it would be for any other thing. Let it be understood that Sex Magick places the sexual act upon a high, idealistic plane. Sex Magick lifts sex play from the low plane to the high plane. Let the critics of Sex Magick understand this well!

Many will ask the question, "What is a good method for attaining proficiency in Alphaism?" A good answer is to practice the Second Degree often. It is not amiss to state in advance that the practice of the Second Degree, Dianism, is innervating and not exhausting in any manner whatsoever, and of course, pleasurably enough to be welcomed by many even every night, for long periods.

XI

TRUMPS Lust

"To lust and enjoy all things of sense and rapture."
To arrive at the peak of magickal ecstasy during
congrex but not to cut it short by "lust for
result"—the orgasm. The longer the ecstasy the more
potent the rite. One should not abandon being in the
arms of the Divine Lover merely to reach the orgasm.
In Crowley's Tarot deck, it is the symbol of sustained
lust in sexual ecstasy.

Reproduced from Aleister Crowley's Tarot deck. Llewellyn
Publications, 1971.

DIANISM: THE SECOND DEGREE

The word *Dianism* refers to the congrex (sexual union) in which the union does not conclude with the orgasmic state. It is not the purpose, per se, in attaining to the Dianism ritual, but rather it is the very necessary method of performing this particular, very potent magickal ritual in order to attain to certain aspired magickal results.

The outstanding thing about the Second Degree is that the sexual congrex does not culminate in a climax. The superficial reader will cry, "That's nothing new. Forty years ago there was a popular book, *Karezza,* which taught that." Any further similarity ends right there. Of the ten points of magick in Dianism, not one was contained in *Karezza.* Worse yet, in *Karezza,* there was no psychologically effective method for preventing frustration because of the no climax rule.

At the early turn of the century there existed the Oneida Community, which practiced the interchange of wives and husbands as a magickal practice, to give a greater unity and spiritual strength to the entire community group. This was excellent magick. The climax was forbidden in these "agape unions" to avoid offspring complications. Because this congrex was held under both the rules of communal love and religious aspiration, there was no resultant frustration because of the absence of the climax. But this was as far as it went. The Oneida

Community was unfortunately short-lived. In those days no group could weather the storm of being charged with "living in sin".

However, the principal denunciation which Dianism must meet is the ignorant charge that Dianism is not a true Western sex magick technic but derives from the Far Eastern Tantric Sex practices.

After giving it due thought, I have decided that the best method is to give a complete account of the sixteen month training curriculum of a high Tantric Master given to his disciples.

The class includes an equal number of men and women aspirants. The first four months are devoted to putting oneself in various positions, or asanas, and holding each position as long as possible without moving. At the same time, several simple geometric designs are used. The procedure is to concentrate the gaze upon one of these designs—to see nothing else—to think of nothing else.

Within six months the group was practicing the classical position for the sexual congrex. The man sits cross-legged on the floor and the woman sits straddled on his lap, facing him. The woman has been practicing the technic of manipulating the interior of the vagina in a contracting, pulsating motion.

As the woman sits on the man's lap facing him, the *Lingham* is inserted in the *Yoni*. They now hold this position, absolutely motionless, with the exception of the interior massaging action of the Yoni. They stare directly and steadily into each other's eyes. The rule is, no climax.

At first, the woman is not proficient enough in the Yoni action to cause any pressing demand for the climax; however, as she becomes more proficient, the man will, on occasion, ask for a stop rest. This is done by uttering a word of many syllables which contains the sound of T and S, in repetition.

Staring into each other's eyes, as they become more practiced, induces a sort of quasi-hypnotic trance.

Then comes the big test at the end of twelve months. The woman partner is now a professional—a real expert in manipulating the interior of the Yoni. The man must go from one to two hours without a climax (no rest), all the while staring steadily into the eyes of the woman. If he reaches a climax the woman reports it and the man must go through another two months of various practices. Incidentally, part of the test is that the man must achieve that state which I choose to call the *Borderland State of Consciousness.*[1]

The intended result of this Tantric Sex Magic is that the man attains various psychic powers, such as predicting the future, thought transference and preception and ability at such things as quasi hypnotism and various other methods to control the minds of tothers.

Where Tantric is carried to the point of climax, the two main objectives are: (1) To make a slave zombie out of some person. (2) To establish a link with some younger person so that the aged, dying, Tantric magician may take over their body upon death—a conscious transition upon death. These objectives are to be questioned.

One can see now that the main objective of Tantric Magic is the attainment of magical powers as an end in themselves. On the other hand, all Western Magick worthy of the name aims at the attainment of various magickal powers, but not as an end in themselves. These magickal powers in turn, can and do serve as aids in accomplishing the Great Work, which is attaining to the Knowledge and Conversation (and final union), of one's own Divine Immortal Self.

1. See the author's *The Complete Magick Curriculum of the Secret Order G∴B∴G∴*, (St. Paul: Llewellyn Publications, 1969.)

The Divine Identity has been called a score of different names. In ancient Egypt man was conceived as a double. The physical body (and its characteristics) was called the *Ku,* meaning 'shadow'; the invisible, immortal, magickal self was called the *Ka.* In ancient Greece among the Magi, the most prevailing name was the *Daemon,* not *demon,* and is still a favorite name among psychologists. What psychiatrist Carl Jung has to say about his own Daemon is most relevant. "Many times I have decided upon a certain course of attitude and of action only to be diverted from it by my Daemon."

In the foregoing comparison of Tantric Magic with Western Magick it can be seen that the outstanding difference between the two is that Western Magick is transcendental Magick. This is to say that the essential aspiration is for self-transcendence—the attainment of a spiritual indentification that transcends the conscious personality.

As said before, there is nothing against the purpose of attaining various magickal powers, but this is not to be regarded as an end in itself. There will be those who ask, "In achieving magickal powers, why must this transcendental business always be included?" The answer to this can be seen easily in this and the following chapter on the technic of Dianism. Here, suffice it to say, that with this aspiration for transcendence, the magick force is greatly increased.

There will be, and should be, the question of what kind of woman partner is most desirable. This applied to both the Second Degree and the Third Degree, Quodosch.[2] Different men have vastly different characters and have different requirements. It is a rare woman who does not

2. The Hebrew word *Quodosch* means 'supreme' or 'holy'. It may be spelled Qodosh, Kodosh, or as above.

need some training or conditioning. In most cases, the man must not be impatient. If he has patience, it may turn out that it was his very patience that enabled him to persist until he had conditioned her, without which he would have missed his chance for having an excellent partner.

Any woman partner who is obsessed with mere sensual pleasure, to the extent that it distracts the male and prevents him from having the necessary concentration and required imagination, is obviously not suitable. Even a frigid woman would be more suitable.

Often a woman who has studied occultism becomes impossible because she has too many preconceived ideas which are not in agreement with her role as a good, cooperative partner. If there is any possible rapport, the woman becomes responsive automatically to the aspiration of the male, and after this has happened, it would then be very easy to give her an explanation and an understanding of the magickal aspects.

One should not overlook the good prospects of a woman who is simple and natural, to whom artificiality is a stranger. Nature! Natural! A woman who is, so to speak, a child of Nature, has the qualities of the feminine principle in Nature. The feminine principle responds to what is projected or initiated by the male principle—responds, nourishes, and sustains even the aspirations and imaginations of the male.

For an illustration of the natural, here is given the experience of a well-known friend of mine. Recently he married a woman who was born and raised on a ranch in Mexico. She had been completely unconditioned by the artificialities of "civilized" city life; she was a child of Nature. In this year of marriage she was 31 years old and had never been married before. Yes, as is common, she had succumbed to the drive and itch for sexual intercourse during her twenties, but bear in mind these were not love affairs but merely sexual affairs.

With her husband, at age 31, it was her first time to have a congrex under the condition of being in love. Being an unspoiled child of Nature, she instinctively (and undoubtedly unconsciously) fulfilled all of the foregoing conditions of so idealizing her mate that she was not conscious of his actual outer personality. She was caught up in the rapture of this idealization, which from an occult point of view is union with one's own Divine Self as objectified in the mate. She therefore became a super Sex Magick partner.

It is better that the congrex be performed in the dark so that the personality of the mate is kept in the background. For the same reason, no words should be spoken, which is always a detraction to some extent. Regardless of what has been customary, let both be completely undressed; besides other cogent reasons, this serves as an interchange of the magnetism of both persons. Let there be first slow, unhurried, and gentle love play before the congrex for at least ten minutes, which gives time to bring up the desired imagination to a more vivid and real state. In fact, let nothing be hurried at any time. It takes, even for the most practiced, some time to bring the imagination to a magickal energized force, and the hurried and very active state prevents this.

By the time of actual union, the individual personalities should be in the background: what remains is two who are, by this time, regarded as almost strangers on one hand, yet well-known and recognizable as vehicles of, at least, the *Demi-gods*—half-Gods.

Of course, slowly arises the sexual sensation, but one should not allow one's consciousness to be captured and enmeshed in this sensation, but rather it should be the fire which feeds and inflames the magickal imagination to the point of subjective reality. One might well have memorized the following words as an aid to this aspiration. The Divine Lover speaks: "I am above you, and in you. My ecstasy is in yours. My Joy is to see your Joy."

The ritualists should now begin to regard each other as the outward manifestation or mirror of one's Guardian Angel. The entire attitude is that the partner has become the actual vehicle of one's own Guardian Angel—the divine, immortal Daemon of oneself—that invisible part of oneself to which one yearns to unite, even though there may be only one in ten thousand that consciously knows this.

Let sexual ecstasy be welcomed rather than quelled, but also let it be the reminder and assurance of the following words: "The sign shall be my ecstasy, the consciousness of the continuity of Existence, the omnipresence of my body." So sayeth the Divine Lover.

In most cases after three congrexes this sign is given, and given with a feeling of benediction of a kind that no priest may ever give to one.

Men and women are divided creatures in that they may have only a dim consciousness of their higher self, yet too often it is entirely unknown. What about this divided state? "I am divided for love's sake: for the chance of union." This sexual union is a sacred ritual devoted to and aspired to in spiritual ecstasy.

I advise again that you allow the ecstasy to be aroused to a high pitch, but instead of indulging in and being obsessed by the sensation, make it the fire of one's energized enthusiasm to attain to the consciousness of the presence of one's own higher self, which is in one sense, one's Divine Lover. As an aid to self-control, so that one does not go over the crest of the wave, keep in mind that your Pure Will—or your Real Will—in whatever you do should not be enmeshed in a lust for result. There should be pure joy and ecstasy in what one is doing rather than a lust for result. When one has a lust for result (climax in this case) then, when the result comes there is always a let down: if one does not have this lust for result, then there never comes an end, and one joyously continues doing one's True Will most satisfactorily.

The True Will is an expression and manifestation of the True Self, the Daemon. The more that one achieves empathy with the Daemon, the more is one inclined to actions and interest that are consonant with the True Will. When one is doing one's True Will, there is less effort and force required for good results. If one examines the import of this statement, one can see that closer rapport with the Daemon indirectly brings increased magickal powers—providing the aims be consonant with one's true nature. If this seems to be an indefinite *if,* let it be said that the only *if* is a very definite one i.e., if the aspirant sincerely aspires to discover the True Self, and to be and to do just that.

Here are some excellent words about the technic and aspiration of Dianism.

> *Hold! Hold! Bear up in thy rapture; fall not in swoon of the excellent kisses. Wisdom says be strong. Then canst thou bear more joy! Be not animal; refine thy rapture. If thou drink, drink by the eight and ninety rules of art; if thou love, exceed by delicacy; if thou do aught joyous, let there be subtlety therein. But exceed!*

At this point, a rather lengthy digression seems exigent. Many readers may become impatient and complain, "What is this anyway! Just a religious ritual?" Indeed it is not. The Dianism rite can well be practiced for a great number of purposes and desires, and with great success, providing that they conform to the conditions which any good psychologist would stipulate i.e., that the objectives or desires be not in conflict with one's own true nature. Every person who is capable of self-honesty will surely know when and how any particular desired objective is alien to their own true, unique self. We all know the metaphorical implication of a tiger foolishly wanting to change his stripes to the spots of the leopard. He could never become a true leopard even if he could change so that he looked exactly like a leopard.

Then why are we treating this apparently religious technic so extensively? Because it is absolutely the essential first accomplishment, for the following reason:

> *(1) It is the only known method in which the participants can sustain the proper amount of extended time needed to get the best results in all phases of the technic.*
>
> *(2) It is the only known technic (for most people) wherein the practice of Dianism does not lead to sexual frustration, but instead leads to complete fulfillment.*
>
> *(3) It in no way leads to a depletion of physical, mental, emotional, and sexual energy, but actually, when well practiced, increases the magickal sexual force.*
>
> *(4) After practicing perhaps six congrexes by this technic, the two performing magicians may be almost totally concentrated in attaining to a different aim or objective, yet this transcendental technic goes on automatically to bring about the desired spiritual growth and union. Thus there are two objectives working at the same time while concentrating on only one of them.*

(5)   Even in the practice of the Third Degree, Quodosch, the foregoing conditions of Dianism will have given the participants the method for carrying this degree to the required length of time for the necessary concentration. Time is required!

(6) This technic produces some most astounding and satisfactory results when used in what is called extended Dianism.

(7) This particular technic gives or induces great suprasensual wisdom or direction in those other desires one may have, even very materialistic desires.

To explain the method for maintaining the proper attitude and imagination without being diverted by the sexual ecstasy, we resort to an illustration. Suppose that you are looking at a most beautiful sunset with colors of red, yellow, and blue in the low hanging clouds. There are two ways that you can respond to this. (1) To be totally engrossed in the beautiful scene—the sensation upon the eyes producing sensual pleasure. (2) This beautiful, ecstatic scene does not completely obsess one in the sensual vision, but rather it is the fire which stimulates and feeds an exalted imagination leading to an ecstatic veneration.

Thus also, must the physical sexual sensation feed the fire of imagination and veneration—the aspiration to unite with soul in ecstasy—and naturally producing the resulting inspiration of being under the presence and benediction of the soul.

Perhaps the first difficulty for the beginner is to envision the technic, seemingly too difficult and complicated, but really very simple. Here follows a summation of injunctions.

(1) The participants should not attempt to delay, quell, or suppress the sexual sensation and pleasure.

(2) There should be no hasty movements or anticipations, but instead all should be calm and easy.

(3) One should not be hoping for the sexual ecstasy to soon arise. It comes soon enough.

(4) One must be neither engrossed in nor obsessed by the sexual ecstasy, though it should be a joyous stimulation.

(5) The sexual ecstasy is to be transmuted into the magickal fire which feeds the ecstasy of being united with s o u l, and is to stimulate the magickal imagination that one is in the arms of the manifestation of one's own Divine Lover—the Guardian Angel, the directing and protecting Daemon, sometimes called the heavenly Bridegroom.

(6) The noticeable result, even as soon as the second congrex, is a very peaceful and contented feeling, a feeling of being blessed by a loving spiritual benediction. The woman partner generally feels this after the very first congrex. This feeling can persist for days.

(7) Besides the fact that no force or energy is lost, one of the great values of Dianism Sex Magick is that there is even a sense of having something added to oneself.

(8) Since there has been no diminution of anything, the readiness of the sexual desire is generally equally as strong as on the preceding congrex night. In anything whatsoever, the injunction is to practice as much as possible. It is well advised that the magicians practice as often as desired and possible. Even the steady regularity of practice has its own ever-increasing magickal power, force, and energy.

(9) There should be no words spoken during the congrex. If one is getting too close to the crest of the

wave, there should be a simple prearranged signal to "be still," such as a gentle pinch. Signals for other things can also be arranged.

(10) Never forget to quell the awareness that one is conjoined with a certain known personality. Let the partner lose all identity, for the coming visualization is that the partner is an objective vehicle of one's own soul—one's Angel.

How long should the congrex last? In the beginning, the ritualists should stop when they are getting tired or when there is a feeling that the magickal force has been exhausted. After each congrex practice the duration of time will be extended. In fact, heavy tiredness should not be felt but rather a feeling of delicious languor and a feeling of spiritual rejuvenation. "Practice often" is a rule for all rituals in Magick, and in this there is a great virtue in Dianism. Without the climax (or any frustration from it), the ritualists will be fresh and ready—and even eager—for the next congrex.

Again I stress the importance that the sexual ecstasy should be welcomed but not indulged in as such. One should direct the sexual ecstasy to one's aspiration, to feed the fire of the ecstasy of being in the love of the Heavenly Lover. It should also be the fire which feeds and energizes the imagination to the point of becoming subjectively real. Incidentally, when all of this is well done, it almost completely dampens the desire for a climax. One has no desire to end the ecstasy of the soul for and by a momentary, physical, climactic quiver of nerves.

When the conditions of the foregoing paragraph are well practiced and repeated with increasing force for five to ten times, then there should result a complex, called the *Bud-Will* or *Magickal Offspring*. Take note that the number of required repetitions depends upon the intensity of the magickal imagination and the concomitant intensity of the desire and aspiration, and even upon the resulting inspiration.

At this point it is well to give a quotation from the greatest master of Magick of this century, Aleister Crowley, miscalled the Chief of the Black Magicians. There are many slanderous accounts in print about Crowley, and we also admit that we cannot approve of many of his actions or his personality. Nevertheless, in the following quotation, note how strict he was in keeping his oath of secrecy never to reveal, in open writing, the secrets of Sex Magick. He wrote cryptically enough so that no one would understand it unless they had previous knowledge of the subject.

> *First, ever be it that you are in the Knowledge of the Holy Guardian Angel. Is it not written in our Book that the Divine Lover gives the assurance that "I am above you and in you. My ecstasy is in yours: My joy is to see your joy. Come, arouse the coiled splendour within you: but ever unto me."*
>
> *You shall aspire to your own true will and all that you desire in Magick is to be consonant with your true nature. Yea, so be it with your "Bud-Will". Formulate this Bud-Will as an Intelligence, a magickal Child, seeking or constructing it, and naming it according to its desired and consonant nature, according to its infallible Rule of Truth.*
>
> *Purify and consecrate this Child, concentrating upon it against other possible intrusions in the operation. This should even continue in your daily life. Make ready for a renewal of this Child in virility and strength.*

Now do this continuously, for by repetition comes forth strength, skill, and also power and intelligence of the Child, if you do not allow time for the force of the operation to dissipate itself before the offspring is complete.

This last paragraph refers to bringing the Bud-Will to a state of what in psychology is called a complex, in which the mental and emotional images that are so intensely initiated (and often enough) become autonomously active, even at times without being consciously set into activity—subconsciously or intuitively as occasion may arise.

In past times there was small distinction made between *imagination* and mere *fancy*—arbitrary or capricious, fanciful associations. However, thanks to the advance in the knowledge of psychology, the word imagination, in its best sense, connotes the exercise of plastic or creative power in which there is a formation of mental and emotional images, which although not present in the objective senses, nevertheless the subjective reality contains within itself the possibility of initiating some objective reality.

Now the person who thinks that Saint Peter is whispering in his ear and telling him to do ridiculous things or to run amuck, thinking that his distorted subjective experience is of actual objective reality, is an unfortunate victum of non-selfdirection. We are referring to a different kind of subjective reality as applied in Magick. The magician directs the imagination in a definite, willed direction: he knows the concomitant subjective reality for what it is—a subjective experience. Of course, he also knows that it can lead, under good magickal direction, to some very real objective reality.

We have now seen that the magickal imagination, in any magickal operation, is to be directed in a specific direction by the intent and will of the magician. The magickal imagination is a willed and directed visualization carried on with such intensity and persistence that in producing such a strong subjective reality, it contains the germ and seed of some objective reality. In this paragraph is a statement of the entire foundation of operational Magick.

It is now exigent to give reference to this condition called subjective reality. Psychologists are acquainted only too well with this state; however, they are concerned almost exclusively with subjective reality in psychopathic cases. It is well to give an exemplar of such, if for no other reason than to show just how real and how potent it can be. Take note however, that in psychopathic cases the imagination is not consciously self-willed and self-directed: this is to say that such a person is a victim of the imagination.

(1) Francis X thought that Saint Peter was frequently talking to him. Saint Peter told him to do some very wrong things and finally Francis X was confined in an asylum.

In this case, there was no intelligent, willed self-direction toward subjective reality, and it, as usual, was thought by him to be objective reality rather than subjective reality.

(2) There were thousands of people who were suffering from what is called psychosomatic illness who, upon drinking the "Sacred Water" from some noted miraculous well or spring, were almost instantaneously cured.

This shows what power there can be in subjective reality when applied to a preceding subjective reality.

But what we are really interested in is that Magick where the magickal imagination is specifically self-directed to attain to a very real subjective reality, which even results in a recognizable objective reality. This technic is reserved for later discussion; however, the foregoing exemplars have served the purpose of showing how powerful the self-directed subjective reality can be and that it can also result in a very real objective reality, when directed by an inspired and maintained magickal imagination.

I know of no better exemplar of this imagination than that given by Aleister Crowley in the essay "Energised Enthusiasm," paraphrased briefly as follows:

When you go to a dance, imagine that all the people at the dance are like angels. I do not mean that you use a sloppy, indifferent imagination. I mean that the imagination is so inspired and so intense that you can see and feel in those people something that is beyond the appearance of their outward visible forms. What you should actually be seeing (though even subconsciously) is the beautiful, divine soul within each person, despite what may be an ugly form when judged by the camera. In fact, you should not be seeing the outer form. Perhaps "angels" do not even have an "outer form" as we know the outer form. You no longer see individual personalities because the total imagination is confined to the spiritually sublime. We may well illustrate this as being much the same as when a person is completely possessed in that first bloom of being in love. It is written, "I remember thy first kiss, even as a maiden should. Nor in the dark byways, is there another. Thy first kiss abides: it was as with an angel."

Now then, at this dance, if there are drinks, imagine that it is the "nectar of the Gods". Imagine the music to be the music of the spheres which touches your actual soul rather than your ears. Do you smell sweat on your partner, weak imaginator? No! It should be transmuted into a perfume that swirls up into the nostrils of the Gods. In your Magickal Imagination you are dancing with no one less than the Goddess Isis, and let her be the outward manifestation of your own Divine Lover, the Secret Center of your Soul, the Guardian Angel immortal, your sacred Daemon.

Have you imagined well, to feel subjective reality, then come home and tell what miracle has happened. There should also be some resulting objective reality.

Think you that this is too "religious" for you? This is not of the religion of edifices built by man, or of denominational creeds. If we must use the word religion, it is the religion of all Living Nature. It is being in rapport with all Living Nature rather than beliefs and faith. It is, therefore, being Natural under Aspiration. The early Greeks called it Pantheism while in Phoenicia the feminine aspect of Pan was Babalon. In the natural veneration for Living Nature, it is quite natural and easy to invoke the required imagination to a point of subjective reality. From the standpoint of being natural as Nature is natural, the imagination is almost natural in itself.

For a further inspired guide to the real imagination, one should reagrd the following quotation from *Liber 31* as the assured words of the Holy Guardian Angel.

> *Come forth, under the stars, and take your fill of love. I am above you and in you. My ecstasy is in yours. My joy is to see your joy. I am divided for love's sake, for the chance of union. And the sign shall be my ecstasy, the consciousness of the continuity of existence, the omnipresence of my body. Be not animal; refine thy rapture. If thou drink, drink by the eight and ninety rules of art: if thou love, exceed by delicacy; and if thou do aught joyous, let there be subtlety therein. But ever unto me—unto me.*

DIANISM ELABORATED

Here follows a synopsis of Dianism.

The Attitude

(1) The required attitude and willed imagination of the man is to lose all possible awareness of the woman partner as a certain person; he must be as impersonal as possible toward her personality.

(2) The man should regard the woman partner (imagined and visualized) as a tangible manifestation of his own Daemon, his Divine Lover, transmuting her.

(3) The woman partner may have a climax only if it does not diminish her continuing enjoyment. She must not be sexually aggressive and should never strive for the climax; striving is out. It is not necessary to inform her in detail, but she should at least be unconsciously receptive to the aspirations of the man, and willing to take the man on his own terms, rather than on any of her terms.

The Sexual Ecstasy

(1) The man should welcome the ecstasy but not indulge in it; rather he should imagine and will that the sexual ecstasy is immediately the continuing fire which feeds the magickal visualization and imagination of being in union with his Soul Lover, his Daemon, and other specific objectives of the rite. When well done, this represses the desire for the climax.

(2) Whatever success results in attaining the Knowledge and Conversation of the Soul Daemon automatically brings other magickal powers that serve directly or indirectly to attaining self-transcendence.

The Climax

(1) In the congrex union the man must not have a climax. The woman partner may have a climax only under certain conditions.

(2) This rite is to be exclusively concerned with its objectives, never lust for the result of climax. To welcome sexual ecstasy without striving. There is no loss of sexual energy and power of ecstasy, thus enabling one to practice often. It gives an increase in energized force.

The Magickal Child

(1) To create what is variously called the magickal complex, the magickal intelligence, the Magickal Child, and the Bud-Will, which continue in time autonomously.

The outstanding difference between the Second Degree and the Third Degree is that there is to be no climax in the Second Degree congrex. This is especially applicable to the male. If the woman partner cannot forego the climax for a long period of time, she does not make a good partner except under one condition, that she can continue with sexual enthusiasm even after having a climax. There are some, however, who are amenable to conforming to your explanations and desires. The woman who is sexually aggressive is, in most cases, almost impossible. She diverts the purpose of the man and also makes it too difficult for him to concentrate upon the magickal imagination.

In the second degree working, there are several good reasons for the no climax rule. In the first place, if the man decides that there shall be no strong desire (or force) for the climax, then there will be no diversion from being exclusively concerned with all of the desired objectives of the rite. Although the union be not carried to the point of a frustrating drive for the climax, nevertheless he can (and should) welcome the sexual ecstasy. However, he should not be diverted by indulging himself in the ecstasy. This ecstasy is to feed the fire of the magickal imagination.

If the woman is also an initiate in the magickal congrex, it is obvious that all rules apply to her as well. Even a half-hour before the actual union, let the man begin to erase, as much as possible, his awareness of the woman as a definitely know personality. The reason for this is that, to begin with, he should regard her as no less than a goddess—for a few minutes. The next step is to imagine her to be a visualized, tangible manifestation of his own Daemon, his Divine Lover.

The following is a ritual that can be done before the congrex begins, to enforce the non-identity of the partner.

The Ritual

The man stands before the woman and says, "Before me, you are a woman known to me as (her name) but in this Great Work of Magick Art I no longer know you by your outer personality."

He touches her shoulder with his hand and says, "You are now the High Priestess of this Art, to give your aid and blessing."

He touches her other shoulder and says, "You are the Queen who gives the royal benediction to this work of Art."

He touches her head and says, "You are a Goddess—a real Goddess—without whose presence there could be no miracle resulting from this rite of Magick."

The ritual need not be actually performed but by some manner must you and your partner be brought to the attitude described in the ritual. Both of you should lose your identity; you must become something else—high ritualists of another world. All of this requires the use of the magickal imagination.

The magician will know instinctively and instantly when his magickal imagination begins to be subjectively real. He will be transformed with a different ecstasy. Incidentally, the woman will also feel transformed and there is then a continuing circle of magickal force.

I have found by practical experience that to give some good case histories is the best method for assuring a clear comprehension of Sex Magick—even down to relevant details. The following case history is one of my own experiences. It is only for the sake of giving an excellent, detailed, and intimate case that I strip myself naked, as it were, before the gaze of many people.

My second marriage was with a native Mexican woman who lived close to the border. She had a short-term pass which allowed her to visit me for two days every week. I was with her for only five weekends before she left for a visit to her father on a ranch, deep in Mexico.

On these visits she would not allow me to kiss or embrace her. She said, "I shall never have any affection for any man: my heart is as hard as a rock." However, in the sex congrex she was very ardent. Here was a puzzle.

I found out from other sources that she had been through three heartbreaking love affairs in the past. I reasoned that because of these experiences she had steeled herself to a point where she was actually not capable of having love and affection for a man, but even so, she could not have completely killed her heart. I therefore decided that the latent potential for love could somehow be awakened. In this case, the decision was that the potential was deep, ardent, affectionate love.

I cannot say that I loved her deeply; she put the damper on that by her steel-willed aloofness. Rather, it was a mixture of affection, a strong fascination, and an intense enchantment. Can the reader see that this was a great force (fire) to help feed the magickal imagination? Lucky is the magician who might have this great magickal stimulation!

We digress to say that if the man has a sense of alertness, awareness, and mental resourcefulness, he might find something to stimulate the energized enthusiasm, issuing from a feeling of the seductiveness of the unusual or from a sense of enchantment. It was from this, and this alone, that I was able to bring the congrex to great results, even though, as you will observe, I was working under other unfavorable and restrictive conditions.

In the first place, my wife, without any preliminaries, set herself to striving for the climax which always came within no more than eight minutes. Under average conditions this is not nearly enough time to get the magickal imagination into good operation. Furthermore, if and when she wanted to continue to another climax, then her physical striving was so energetic that it made any concentration almost impossible. In short, had I not been aided by all that was mentioned so far, it would have been a futile operation.

Being in a state of enchantment it was easy to visualize her as a goddess and then as a tangible manifestation of the Heavenly Lover, my Daemon, within four minutes of the operation. The other objective led from my conviction that she had a great potential for love, even though almost completely repressed to inactivity; therefore, the magickal invocation was love.

The congrex series was only for five consecutive weekends before her trip to visit her relatives on a secluded ranch in Zacatecas, Mexico. On the morning that she left she kissed me for the first time. I shall always remember that kiss, as long as I live. I said, "Darling, you told me that you could not love any man, but you love me."

She answered, "With all my heart I love you." That was when I knew that the Bud-Will, the Magickal Offspring had been generated. But the operation had been exclusively for her and I knew for certain that she was leaving with a part of me.

On the eighth day of her departure, it hit me. I knew that I had lost my wife—how, I did not know. In checking on all details at a later date, it turned out that the day and hour that I knew that I had lost her was the identical time that she had been murdered. For two months I was like a walking zombie for she had taken a part of myself with her. In desperation to recover something, I set out to visit her father and sister.

The final result from the Magickal Offspring was when some weeks later, I received a letter from her sister. The pertinent part read, "There is something about you and my sister that is in this ranch house. It finally comes strong to me that I love you and I know that you love me. I have to stay here at the ranch to help out for a few months and I will be waiting for you to come down and marry me and take me back with you."

This is an incredible outcome except for the magickal explanation. Knowing all of the details as I do, the evidence is that there still had been a persisting force of the magickal intelligence that was with my wife.

A final note on this is that the successful creation of the Bud-Will is a special part of the Third Degree instead of the Second Degree. There are certain operations in the Third Degree that are supposed to be essential for this. But none of this was done in this particular case. That is why this exemplar has been included under the Second Degree.

The gross materialist says, "If I want to get magickal powers, then why must I also invoke this entity that you call one's Daemon, as Carl Jung also calls it?" My answer has always been that to achieve the necessary energized enthusiasm and magickal imagination, it is almost a must for most neophyte operators. Thus it was with 75 per cent of my record cases—failure to conjure up enough force. In what might be called successful cases when first observed, the kind of magickal powers invoked were not consonant with one's own true self and in the end, the use of these powers boomeranged and were bitter as gall in the stomach.

Others have said, "I do not believe in any existence whatsoever of this Daemon or whatever name you give it even though Dr. Carl Jung and a thousand mystics and magicians testify to its existence." My answer has always been that if you can admit the existence of any intelligence, visible or invisible, that is superior to yourself, then proceed just as you have been. If you cannot be sincere you should not monkey with Magick. But if you can sincerely operate and imagine as directed, you will be convinced about your Daemon. Atheists are a hard-headed lot and only a few follow through, but of those who do, many are convinced, and when an atheist will give up his determined negation, that is something!

The big joke is that when the magician practices often and in aspiration to self-transcendence, then it is not necessary to invoke magickal powers. All magickal powers that are consonant with one's unique nature in relation to the Guardian Angel are automatically given—those powers that are of most value for the attainment of the Great Work.

The trance in Dianism is a technic in which the congrex lasts from two to four hours, depending on the conditions. The objective of this method is to achieve the Borderland

State of Consciousness. This is very much the same as that borderland state where one is neither completely awake nor completely asleep. Dreams occur when one is about 75 per cent asleep and 25 per cent awake. In the trance congrex it is about 50-50. To move into this state, the body motions slow down at the same time that the conscious awareness lessens.

After one successful trance operation, one man was able to arrive at the state of subjective reality of the magickal imagination in one-half the time that he had previously needed. He thereby soon attained to the sphere of Tiphareth, which in the language of the citadels of Western Sex Magick, implies that he had accomplished the brilliant realization of the Knowledge and Conversation of the Guardian Angel. This prepared him for the next grade in the Great Work which is attaining the actual union with the Angel. (This is bringing the conscious self to a state of transcendence where there is a conscious union with the Heavenly Lover, the Daemon.)

During the last part of a trance, I once saw clearly how to work with certain obscure keys in the Yi King (also spelled I Ching) and how to bring the Yi King up to its original intent. (Both Legge and Wilhelm knew about these keys, but instead of proceeding from there, they based their writings upon the writings of King Wan and later masters and these are hardly better than 60 per cent correct.) The use of the Yi King in Magick is very great. The reader will note that what came to me on the Yi was a case of reading in the World of Mind and is one of the valuable magickal powers, especially in magickal operations. As said before, it should be stressed that one gets magickal powers that are related to one's needs and which are also consonant with one's nature, automatically i.e., without any specific invocation of these powers. This applies to all workings in the Second Degree. In the Third

Degree, where there is no specific invocation of magickal powers, it applies also—even stronger.

A well-practiced magician had been neglecting his social life. Moreover, he suddenly came to the point where he wanted to have a good wife, but he knew of no prospects. He invoked the power to attract the interest of women. In his magickal imagination he envisioned himself as asking a woman to marry him within only five minutes of meeting her—if he was attracted to her. The first woman he was attracted to said yes to the question, "How would you like to marry me?" after only five minutes of acquaintanceship. He got exactly what he had asked for in his invocation but other things developed which made it turn sour very quickly. After all, his invocation was not to get a good wife. Within a period of four months, there were seven women who had said yes within five minutes, but none were good prospects for a suitable wife.

By that time, our hero got the message and constructed the invocation to include a good and suitable wife having mutual affection. By this time five minutes was a habit, nevertheless, it was a happy and affectionate marriage.

Let the reader study all these exemplars. He can glean many very valuable points graphically.

The Dianism trance is carried to a point in time when the two partners slow down to an almost motionless state of delicious languor and then continue down to a near dreamy state. Then there will come marvelous inspirations, almost visionlike, and there will even come from afar the assurance that it is no mere imagination that one is in the loving, protecting arms of one's Lover Daemon. There are all kinds of scintillating variations of result. These results can, to a large extent, be directed in accordance with one's aspirations or desires, even materialistic results which are consonant with one's needs in the Great Work.

Here is a good example of how to direct the result. I had been living for two months in unsettled country and needed water. I assiduously dug for water in various places with no results. I asked for the blessing of the Daemon in the form of the suprasensual psychic mind to locate water, in the extended Dianism rite. Close to the termination of the rite I had a vision of the exact location to dig for water. On the following morning I located an underground spring flow at the astounding dept of only five feet.

To summarize, the various things that can be accomplished by Dianism (normal and extended) are any that do not require the specific application of the Third Degree, Quodosch. There is however an overlapping. Some things can be accomplished by both methods, but there are some things that are more easily and better accomplished by the Quodosch method and others by the Dianism method. Identification with the Angel is as important in Quodosch as in Dianism, as is also the submergence of the identity of the personality of the partner, at least partially. The soul or Angel is not identifiable as a personality as we conceive of personality.

Depending upon the magicians and their experience, this extended Dianism rite, carried to the point of a slight trancelike state or what I call the Borderland State, will seldom require less than one hour and most often two or three hours.

I mentioned the skeptic who says, "I do not believe in the existence of the Daemon, or the Heavenly Lover, or whatever you wish to call it." I challenge the skeptic to sincerely practice this rite until he attains to the Borderland State. He (or she) will have inspiring visions and possibly even a caress of the Angel—if he is not completely beyond redemption!

In any event, to all aspiring ones, spiritual vision and transcendent illumination are guaranteed, though at first it may be delicious languor and that feeling of love and peace which transcends daily life.

The Star

When correctly drawn, this card shows one jug dipping water from the ocean and the other pouring water that has been so dipped onto the ground where it trickles back to its source, the ocean. There is an expression in Crowley's Gnostic Mass "Without diminution of substances or loss of effulgence". In Quodosch, there is no feeling of loss after the orgasm. The star overhead is the Seven Pointed Star of Babalon—the Great Mother of Sex Magick and the feminine aspect of Pan.

Reproduced from Aleister Crowley's Tarot Deck. Llewellyn Publications, 1971.

QUODOSCH: THE THIRD DEGREE

When the reader scans a short list of suggested uses for the Third Degree, he should be able to see that the Second Degree is equally applicable though not as potent. In other cases the work comes exclusively under the Third Degree. If one depends on a letter to influence the recipient, then what better method could there be than to "charge" the letter with the force of one's will, which in the case of Sex Magick would be to dribble the letter with the actual quintessence which had been charged with the magick intent!

If one should desire to bring soul transcendence to the woman partner, one cannot imagine anything more potent than to feed some of the transmuted quintessence to her! We have the rule to practice often. Well then, consider the fact that much can be accomplished to this end in the Second Degree congrex. Consider well the idea of interspersing the Second Degree rite with the Third Degree rite. This is of great value because the partners do not become tired by frequent repetition. There are few people who can perform frequent repetitions in the Third Degree alone, without diminishing both the energized enthusiasm and the magickal imagination. Discretion and selectivity should be the watchwords.

The greater the power that anything has for good use, the greater the power it has for misuse. But here is a guarantee. If the budding magician follows all the rules given in this text, with sincerity in practice, then nothing will harmfully explode.

Remember that "Every man and every woman is a star." Each one is potentially unique and going in its own orbit. It is not eccentricity, but an abiding aspiration to discover your own unique individuality. This is the heart of all transcendental Magick.

I have received so many plaints about getting a suitable partner that I have decided to give a special exemplar. In this case, the husband and wife were incompatible and they had agreed to separate within thirty days. He, being a brother member in a secret magickal order, had high aspirations in the Great Work. Due to his frustration he had an intense desire to have a suitable magickal partner for the congrex workings; therefore, even though his wife was not a good partner, the very intensity of his desire served much to overcome the incompatibility between them, in assaying to create the Bud-Will Intelligence to have a good partner.

After five congrexes he was certain that he had given autonomous intelligence to the Bud-Will, and that is where his story begins.

He insisted that he write the story himself, and for the sake of anonymity he even used my name, Lou. I lived close by and intimately knew all of the principles involved, so well that it almost feels like my own experience.

Before giving his account, it is exigent to make a strong point about the necessity in all Magick to be continually aware. The magician should swear the oath of intent, "I swear to regard every incident as a possible dealing between myself and my Daemon and his messenger, the Bud-Will Intelligence." Awareness, vigilance, awareness! Let the reader see that if "Lou" had not been vigilant when he first saw "Alice," he would not have recognized the sign of the working of his Bud-Will Intelligence and there would have been the possibility of his magickal work going for nought. Indeed, it seems to me to be poetic justice that one does not deserve any good outcome from his active desires if he or she is too indifferent to be ever vigilant for any possible encouraging sign.

Here follows the exemplar in the subject's own words.

I was driving from Fallbrook with grocery supplies for my place in Rainbow Valley. Halfway home there was a woman thumbing a ride. I never pick up hitchhikers so I did not stop. Suddenly it hit me: there was something about the way we exchanged glances that struck me as a possible sign. I stoped about a hundred yards past her. She disdained another car that had stopped and started to walk rapidly to my car and eagerly entered it.

She said, "I have to get home to San Bernardino to take care of my two kids. Was at a family reunion in San Diego. All of 'em drunk yesterday and all night and I ain't had no sleep and nothing to eat. Here I am, chattering like a guinea hen and ain't even told you my name. Name's Alice, born in the Ozark Mountains of Arkansas."

Suddenly her head dropped heavy on my shoulder and she was asleep. In turning from the main road and going to my place, the jolting of the car woke her.

"Where are we at?" she asked.

I said, "We are going to my place and while you are having some sleep I am going to cook a steak for you and then I'll buy you a ticket for San Berdou."

She looked at me through the eyes of 100 per cent woman and said, "Lou, I must be dreaming: you are such a swell guy."

After eating she flopped on the bed again and was asleep within a minute. When I awakened her she said that she could get the midnight bus. "Kiss me, Lou," she said.

"Ever since I had titties I have dreamed about being loved by a man like you. Let's take our clothes off and you just love me. That's all: no sex."

But the gods (and the Bud-Will) work in devious ways. She said that it would be soon enough to take the early morning bus. *"Crimonetly! Tain't no good being treated like I was an angel by a man like you that I could worship. I just got to be loved by you, all the way, even if only once. Take me, Lou."*

On the following morning she said, *"You've taken me up almost to heaven and now I am dropped back down to earth. It hurts like hell to fall so hard. I know you are not for me no more. My old man gets out of jail next week and I have to be with him. But Lou, I am going to do something for you. I am going to give you my sister. Up till two weeks ago she was raised in the Ozarks by Granny. Then she came here to drunken Ma. Only seventeen and nobody to take care of her. And I seen some of those Berdou dudes sniffing around. You are the only man in the whole world I'd trust to have her."*

I was too stunned to say anything. We went to the only store in the valley, Ed's Grocery and Eatery to wait for the bus. After we had ordered a cup of coffee, Alice went behind the counter and was talking to Ed in a low voice. Then she told me, *"I see you're poke flat for money and I asked him if he would give part-time work to my sister Mabel. He said yes, he needs her."*

Only three days passed before Alice brought Mabel down in a borrowed car. When Alice drove away I said, *"Well, that is a switch. The Lord giveth and the Lord taketh away, but here the Lord is giving something back even better."*

Mabel did not know what I meant but on the morning after the second night she said to me, *"The Lord shore* gives." And the Lord gave on many succeeding nights, according to Mabel.

I raised hand-tamed animals on my place and one day a dude from San Diego came to Ed's place inquiring about the ranch. The dude's uncle wanted him to put down a deposit on a pair of wolf pups.

Mabel was just getting ready to leave the restaurant to go back to the ranch. She said to the dude, "Lou ain't in today but he lets me handle his business. Give me $100 for a deposit."

But the dude was looking her over, with ideas. He said, "I want to see those wolves first."

"Let's go," said Mabel.

The dude whispered to Ed, "I'm going to get some of that stuff."

At first the dude played it cautious but it was enough to give Mabel suspicions and she planted her legs apart and gave him a taunting laugh.

"I forget what I first said to her," the dude told Ed, "but she just stared at me with a smile and said, 'I am a one man woman.' Then I got my arms around her and said 'Don't play it coy baby. Gorgeous stuff like you has been had by plenty of men.' Then she yelped, 'You hadn't auta said that!' and she came up with her leg and gave me the knee right in my knockers—hard. Cripes that hurt."

Ed laughed in derision. "More ambition than good judgement."

I think that I have the best magickal congrex partner in the world. I married her, but not because I wanted to own her. She was a precious gift which should not be owned.

The reader of this exemplar will do better to trace the workings of the Bud-Will Intelligence for himself than to have it outlined for him. It is clear enough. May this experience inspire others to work for a magickal partner

*rather than wishing for it, and also to be resourceful and
patient enough to train her, and to treasure her when you
get her. This is my hope and advice.*

We now find it useful to employ some of the symbology
of Alchemy and the Tree of Life. If we go back far enough
we are assured that the word *Alchemy* derives from the
Arabic word *Al-kimiya.* Some of the early writings on
Alchemy contained disguised secrets of Sufi Sex Magick.
Naturally, it can be seen that many writings on Alchemy
were records of practicing alchemists for transmuting
various base elements into rare or more valuable chemicals,
and also of medicinal experiments such as those conducted
by Theophrastus Bombastus von Hoenheim—Paracelsus.

The magick of Alchemy, per se, is well illustrated in the
Hans Olsen case. I had watched him put hundreds of
batches of different ingredients through his furnace. He
was actually trying to make rare metals out of the base
metals. It became for him a magickal ritual in which, both
consciously and unconsciously, he was associating it with
refining and developing his higher potentiality. The result
was the he actually attained to a very real initiation. His
reasoning, or insight on the material plane even became
charged, and under inspiration he developed a waterproof
cement by a method which other cement chemists of high
standing said was impossible.

Even in the cultivation of one's garden a magickal ritual
may be employed. The cultivation of the plants is also seen
with the magickal imagination as an outward act of
developing one's spiritual forces. It would also seem that it
was a person of some magickal understanding who created
the creed of the Church of England concerning the
Eucharist as "An outward and visible act as a Token of an
inward and spiritual grace."

The Alchemic Symbols

Cucurbit: The Female organ, per se.

The Alembic Retort: The same organ in process of transmutation.

Menstruum: The magick solvent of the female organ.

The Eagle: The female.

The White Eagle: Same as the menstruum.

The Lion: The male.

The Red Lion: The male essence.

Sublimate: Not as misused in modern language which conveys the idea of a substitute for the sexual act, but in the alchemic meaning to exalt and to refine. The physical that is prepared for transmutation.

Transmutation: Metaphorically changing base metal to gold. Physical ecstasy transmuted to spiritual ecstasy.

Elexir: The Red Lion sexual essence.

Quintessence: The transmuted elexir.

Transubstantiation: In various religions this is the magickal process of the "flesh and blood" of the god being present in the consecrated bread and wine. This practice is vulgarly but significantly called God eating.

The Mother Eagle: The mucous membranes, as in the female vulva and in the mouth of the Eagle and Lion.

Words relating to the Tree of Life

Yesod: Simple, instinctive union with the feelings and emotions.

Tiphareth: The Knowledge and Conversation of the Holy Guardian Angel. This is below the grade of actual union or identification.

Chokmah: Masculine wisdom; wisdom being positive male.

Binah: Feminine understanding; understanding; receptive repository.

The Abyss: A psychic disaster for the presumptuous, unworthy person. Only a sincere person should chance the oath of crossing the abyss.

Kether: That high sphere where the wisdom of men is foolishness with the gods and the wisdom of the gods is foolishness with men. Here is the great key of the aphorism given forth by Crowley, "No idea is worth entertaining unless it can be seen where and how the opposite is equally true." Even beauty and its opposite, ugliness, must, in Kether, merge into a higher principle which transcends both.

Everything that has been given in the Second Degree, Dianism, is included in the Quodosch practice, except that the rule in Dianism is no climax. It is therefore not necessary to repeat all that was given in Dianism.

In a complete sexual union there may result the generation of a physical offspring. For practical purposes we may assume that whether a child is conceived or not, there is a psychic result from each and every sexual union. For the convenience of language, we may call this a Magickal Offspring. Just what is meant by Magickal Offspring? It is better that this text, as it progresses, makes this more clear to both understanding and to experience. In the beginning, let it be understood as a very real manifested psychic result, varying in intensity (subjective reality) according to the willed purpose and direction of the union.

In summary, the essential difference between Quodosch and Dianism is the conjoined menstruum of the White Eagle and the essence of the Red Lion, which under proper operation, has been transmuted to the quintessence which is preserved for a period in the Mother Eagle.

The virtue of the Mother Eagle process is best illustrated with an outstanding example. Anyone may test this. Get six oysters in the shell, alive. Masticate one for a full five minutes before swallowing. Repeat this with the other five oysters, the whole process requiring thirty minutes. The result will be that one is almost drunk with the vital force that has been absorbed directly into the bloodstream through the mucous membrane. Had the oysters been immediately swallowed, the various internal digestive juices and acids would have destroyed this vital force during the activity of breaking down the food for physical nourishment.

There comes a question of the amount of time required in the Mother Eagle: fifteen minutes is generally sufficient, although many times much less time is required.

Now that one is acquainted with certain relevant words in the alchemic idiom, one has sufficient clues to decipher a sample, old alchemical writing. There is some evidence that it was written by Basil Valentine, author of the erudite alchemic work, *The Chariot of Antimony.* Incidentally, one may get enough clues to at least partially decipher an old set of very cryptic drawings under the title of "Splendour Solis".

The Great Alchemical Work

Let the Lion and the Eagle duly prepare themselves as Prince and Princess of Alchemy—as they may be inspired. Let the union of the Red Lion and the White Eagle be neither in cold nor in heat. Let their working be sublimated. Now then comes the time that the elexir is placed in the alembic retort to be subjected to the gentle warmth of the menstruum. The wise alchemist knows the required time in the alembic retort for the transmutation—the medicine of metals, the royal antimony, the quintessence. If the "Great Work" be transubstantiation, then the Red

Lion may feed upon the flesh and blood of the God, and also let the Red Lion duly feed the White Eagle—yea, may the Mother Eagle give sustainment and guard the inner Life.

It is testified that, in special operations desired by the Lion and Eagle, there is unfailing great virtue and force in employing the Anointing Ritual, be it on a letter, a talisman, a magick sigil, a special object of desire, a symbol of aspiration, or upon living flesh.

A word is in order about the natural reaction of most people to those things which are different from their customary thoughts, emotions, and actions. If it is different enough, the emotions, and consequently the mind, regard it as something mysterious and even weird. Then comes the final conclusion that if it is so different from general custom, then it must be evil. Some will also say that it must be dangerous.

Here is the answer—a fact. Any method which may be employed with the basic end in view of attaining a closer awareness of the Divine Spirit or attaining to the Knowledge and Conversation of the Guardian Angel, performed in due aspiration, cannot possibly be evil or wicked.

It is the male Lion who is in command of the process of putting the quintessence into the care of the absorbing Mother Eagle i.e., the various mucous membranes, and therefore the Lion should have a conscience about making an undue imposition upon the Eagle when the operation is entirely for the benefit of the Lion.

Before covering the technic of bringing Intelligences, the Familiar, etc., to light, it is better to give descriptions of other workings of Sex Magick.

First, the Zelator should be reminded that he or she now must have a double concentration and magickal imagination. The Zelator must perform the congrex with all of the attitudes set forth in the Second Degree. Besides this, it is necessary to concentrate on the object desired. Here are several suggested applications.

(1) The letter method. This is to be used in cases where a letter to a particular person has the potential for accomplishing a given purpose. Concentrate on the desired purpose during the congrex. Place a quantity of the quintessence upon the written letter and immediately seal the envelope. Mail it as soon as convenient. I and my associates in Magick can testify that we have never seen this fail in bringing about some result. If another letter is advisable, it should be treated in the same manner. The force is augmented if one traces with the elixir some kind of sigil or symbol which pertains to the objective.

(2) The money method. Applicable where some objective is desired concerning money or a check; also to bring money. Proceed exactly as given in the letter method.

(3) For mental and emotional improvement. To attain such qualities and abilities as joy, concentration, imagination, love, awareness, wisdom, understanding, and many others. Keep the mood of the Second Degree and also concentrate upon the particular propensity desired. Keep it specific and do not allow the mind to wander. Whether the quintessence is preserved via the Mother Eagle of the man or by the Mother Eagle of the woman is a matter of judgement and decision. If the objective is solely for the woman the virtue of the operation is enhanced by tracing an appropriate symbol upon her skin with some of the "medicine of metals". Again, it is well to repeat that the elixir should remain in the cucurbit for a few minutes.

(4) Divination. All serious workers of Magick are desirous of attaining ability in divination (or should

be). The most favored methods, beginning with the most simple are tea leaves, playing cards, Tarot cards, Horary Astrology, and the Yi King. (The Yi King is the most definite, reliable, and in being less tricky, does not require so much so-called psychic ability.) There is also the more direct method of depending upon one's psychic propensitites: this requires the development of the faculty of awareness which is given separately in method number five.

The Zelator should choose one definite method of divination for the magick working. Let him devise a chosen symbol for this method. It is assumed that both partners in the congrex welcome development in this divinatory ability and therefore both are involved in taking part in the absorption of the magick elexir. (On a prepared paper may also be traced the symbol and upon the forehead of both operators.) During the congrex working do not fail to visualize the symbol and the working of the divination. As in all of these magick workings, added strength and wisdom is attained by several repetitions of the magick congrex working.

(5) Awareness. Awareness is of first degree important in all magick working. The mind should be attentively aware of anything that comes to one's sight or feelings so the sight and feelings must also be alert and aware! When a person seeks knowledge, guidance, and future indications, be it by either one of the oracular methods or by the psychic faculties, it may be some very small, apparently insignificant thing which is the key and clue to guidance, and in order to recognize this, a keen and active sense of awareness is required. The magick technic in the congrex is the same as given in method number four.

(6) The attainment of the Knowledge and Conversation of the Holy Guardian Angel. The Holy Guardian Angel is also called the Daemon, the Divine Ego, the Divine Genius,

the Immortal Self, the All-Knower, the One that Goes, and the True Inner Guidance. One should review the required attitude as given in the Second Degree. Dianism: this is very important. Do not identify the partner as a known person; the partner must be identified as an actual manifestation of the Daemon, one's divine self, yet be as a lover!

The central aim of all Magick should be to attain the Knowledge and Conversation of one's Daemon, and prosper chance, finally actual union. This is the true definition of initiation—to discover one's true identity and thereby fulfill the purpose of one's existence on this planet.

Then what about the magickal powers as given in the first five classifications? What better reason is there than to aid one in this Great Work, as it is called! Actually, if one confines the congrex to this central aim, there comes, automatically, enough magick powers for many aspirants, though not specifically so.

The attitude of the magicians is described in the Second Degree. The partner is no longer a certain known person but rather has become a spiritualized manifestation of the Divine Daemon. The whole congrex is as an enchanted spiritual feeling. Let one imagine, realistically, that the Divine Presence communicates, "I am above you and in you. I am here and now with you. My ecstasy is in yours. My joy is to see your joy. I love you: I love you. Come unto me. To me. Thou art verily with me." The aspirants should really feel the benediction of the spiritual presence, and it should persist long after the congrex.

If the aspirants have felt nothing it is due to one of three things: (1) Inhibitions, (2) not capable of spiritual feeling, (3) more practice is needed. Every human endeavor improves and develops by practice.

The results of this magickal rite ever increase with continued practice and even lead to an initiation. No sexual congrex should take place without this rite; the physical, psychological, and spiritual benediction is too great to be neglected.

The Rite of Transubstantiation is naturally the summation of this ritual. In the Christian church the consecrated wine and wafer are declared to be the body and blood of Jesus Christ. The only difference in the herein described magickal rite is that there is an actual vital spiritualized substance that is consecrated. This is a sufficient hint to the wise: to the troglodytes, the whole subject of Magick must remain as an ignorance which even results in their anathema.

The subject is now closed with the following comment by a medical doctor who is also a practicing psychiatrist.

Too many people will object to Sex Magick upon the grounds that the sexual act is supposed to be solely for procreation. They base their argument upon the sex life of animals, saying that animals copulate only during the menstrual season, resulting in procreation. Very well, if they want to base the argument upon physical phenomena and ignore the spiritual and psychological part, let us meet them upon their own ground.

Animals (excepting monkeys) can produce offspring only when the union occurs during the menstrual period or so-called season, but with humans, copulation during the menstrual period is the one time that it is impossible to produce offspring. Thus we see that it is impossible to make a human-animal comparison based exclusively upon physical phenomena. Incidentally, the one exception mentioned, monkeys, happens to be much the same as humans in sexual habits—the same as so many humans whose physical ways occlude the qualities of soul.

The sexual mores of the ancient primitives are illuminating. The most ancient primitives extant in the world are the natives of the Isle of Melville, off the northern coast of Australia, and secondly the natives of the Isle of Iffia. Both of these peoples have a natural instinct to celebrate sacred sexual rituals. So it also goes with the primitives of lesser age and lesser succeeding age until it finally degenerates into mere sexual orgies, just as do modern humans. Strangely enough, it is just this class of humans which is most inclined to decry any idea of associating spirituality with the sexual act. But not so strange either as it is merely a left-handed way of showing their subconscious guilt of practicing the mere gross physical act.

I also find it interesting to observe the instinct for hygiene in the primitives as, for example, the use of a small sponge soaked with the juice of some fruit or plant which is acidic, such as lemon juice. It really is a mystery to me how the so-called teenagers come by their information, such as using a warm bottle of acidic drink such as Seven-Up or Coke as a contraceptive.

In conclusion, let us not overlook the fact that one of the reasons that Sex Magick has been under the cloak of vowed secrecy is that it inevitably would meet with derision, accusations, feigned horror, and persecution by that great mass, the Troglodytes.

(Name withheld by request)

(7) The Bud-Will Intelligence. This has been reserved for closing. The secret of this operation was given only to the few who had been tried and proven, especially as to being greatly proficient in all phases of Dianism.

It has been called the generation of the Magickal Offspring, of the Magickal Child. In some ways, a better name is the Bud-Will Intelligence. The idea of the Magickal Child puzzles one and even repels and frightens some; therefore, it is exigent to give an explanation from modern psychology.

In the language of psychology, the manifestation is called a complex. "A complex is any group of ideas and feelings, heavily charged with energy (conscious or unconscious) that is capable of functioning autonomously to influence personality and general behavior in its own characteristic way." Now it will be seen that when this is unconscious in the subject, it only too often indicates a psychopathic personality.

However, the general public is wrong in assuming that a complex is always subversive. Under certain conditions it can be quite the opposite.

There is one condition in which the complex is the result of a grea magickal achievement. Under cogent and willed creation it aids and serves and even informs the individual, even to the point of genius.

Let one again read the definition of the complex. Take note that it functions autonomously i.e., as an existing, functioning intelligence, apart from one's own thinking state. When one creates or generates this functioning intelligence, it has the actual subjective reality of being a Magickal Offspring and it is both good psychology and good Magick to regard it as an autonomous intelligence, apart and separate from oneself, albeit also an extracted and generated part of oneself.

Here is the tremendous value of the Child. For example, you have concentrated on beauty as its outstanding characteristic. Although it is generated from your microcosmic principle of beauty, it becomes greatly magnified and specialized and communicates to you an infinitely greater sense of beauty than you ever had conceived of consciously.

Note the definition says that it is "heavily charged with energy." There is nothing equal to the force of charging by Sex Magick.

When the Child is for only one of the partners in the congrex, then the same method is used as was given for the oysters. There are cases where both partners are in agreement in these magickal operations, albeit great results have been achieved even when one of the partners was not even aware of the magickal intent.

In ancient times among the Semitic peoples were certain initiates who practiced a certain form of Sex Magick that has some parallels to the various technics as given in this text. One such practice is well recorded. At the time of the sexual congrex the husband would concentrate on the nature of the child to be born. Then when the child reached puberty the father would pronounce his blessing upon the son. These blessings seemed to be predictions for the son, but in reality they were a repetition of what had been concentrated upon and willed at the time of the hoped for conception.

The other special practice is what the anthropologists call the God Eater. In uninitiated practice any substance was consecrated and declared to be a part of the body of God and it was then eaten with the idea of attaining godlike knowledge or power. However, real initiates did not use just any substance. They used what has been described as "neither alive nor dead," i.e., the orgasmic secretion, the semen or sperm which first was receiving the "gentle heat of the cucurbit," i.e., inside the female vulva from which was recovered and consumed by both the male and female—the Lion and the Eagle.

There is much doubt that these ancient magicians knew anything about the technic of transmuting this effluvium into the elexir, or quintessence. However, eventually a few were bound to stumble upon the technic in an intuitive or instinctive way and finally it became a very secret practice.

In my correspondence with Aleister Crowley, he wrote to me, "I know of nothing more distasteful than the first matter (the non-transmuted substance) but the elexir quintessence when transmuted is as of the nectar of the Gods." And this is quite factual.

It is to be supposed that almost everyone knows about the medicinal use of both sublingual capsules and injections of concentrated sexual substance for the purpose of sexual regeneration. Now this is not the essential purpose of Sex Magick as given in this document. The real magickal use of the quintessence is fully outlined here and is not used for any direct purpose of sexual rejuvenation for several reasons. In the first place, the magickal sex congrex, when performed properly as herein given, instead of depleting the performers in any fashion is sexually rejuvenating even without partaking of the elexir, and this has been definitely proven in the Dianism ritual in which there is no resulting physical excretion. In the Quodosch rite there results an actual sexual rejuvenation whether intended for such or not, but as stated, this is not the basic purpose.

Just how and why this Magick produces unfailing results is hardly a matter for theory or speculation because one can become easily diverted by being concerned with mental speculation. The real thing that counts is that it works.

I personally know of many cases where a letter has been written to produce a certain result, in which the desired result was improbable, but when the letter was dribbled with some of the elexir (designed for that purpose) the results were astounding. This applies to all of the various aims in Sex Magick as outlined in this document.

Once again, I am forced to repeat the injunction that Sex Magick should fundamentally contain the invocation to the "bornless one," the H∴G∴A∴, the Daemon.

THE MAGICKAL CHILD

I have received many different letters from readers of my book, *The Complete Magick Curriculum of the Secret Order G∴B∴G∴*, but 75 percent have been requests for more details on the subject of the Magickal Child. For this reason I am devoting this chapter to this particular subject.

The ancient Semites (Arabs, Hebrews, Phoenicians and Egyptians) were the race deeply involved in Sex Magick. You remember the account of the noted Jewish patriarch who pronounced his blessing upon his sons—what they would be, who they would be, and how they would become it. What he actually was doing was repeating his magickal will held at the time of their conception. In other words, he was practicing Sex Magick in the act of making his wife conceive. Thus we see that, in such a case, the Magickal Child was an actual living person. This is what will be covered more explicitly in this chapter.

In that remarkable, most secret doctrine in the book called *Le Compte de Gabalis,* the Magickal Child was a created (or rather invoked) "Elemental" which could (by continued magickal practice) be made "human and immortal like Man." We shall also treat this very cryptic description.

Now the great exponent of Sex Magick, Aleister Crowley, also wrote very cryptically and moreover, he wrote from two standpoints which can easily confuse one.

He often wrote in a metaphorical way which is not to be taken literally. He had a tremendous force of magickal imagination and what he advises or writes of is often not applicable at all to myself or any other average practitioner of Magick. In the "Paris Workings" and also in his work in the desert called *The Vision and the Voice,* Crowley practiced homosexual magick which led him to write from this standpoint in some places which are not applicable in this manual. This has created a problem for me, the writer. I wanted to quote from Crowley for his hidden value which can be deceptive to most of us. Therefore, in this chapter in particular where the partners are of the opposite sex, I beg the reader to allow what is in this chapter to take precedence over some of the things which he wrote which are apparently bald contradictions. In other words, please consider the fact that this chapter is restricted to the Sex Magick between man and woman—opposite polarity—in conformity with Nature's Law and is not concerned with deviations from it.

There have been many names given to the end result of this operation: Magickal Child, Magickal Offspring, Psychic Offspring, Psychic Force, Autonomous Intelligence or Force, Demi-Angel, Elemental, Jinni. Why are there so many names? For the simple reason that there are eight possible different evocations and invocations and eight different willed manifestations, all of which are covered in this chapter.

Crowley has stated that it is not necessary for the woman to be aware of what the man is doing and also that she need not be a person of high development. I say that because of Crowley's great power of magickal imagination and his great magick power and force, that what he says, although applicable to himself, does not apply to most aspiring magicians. Very few, if any, can be a Crowley.

I say that there should be a rapport between the man and the woman and if this is not apparent then one should try to develop the rapport. I also say that the woman should be regarded as one's "magickal instrument," cherished and guarded as one does his other "magickal instruments" and most certainly not to be "adulterated" or "contaminated" by some other man.

On this point I remember when Frater∴132∴ was head of the O.T.O. in Los Angeles. In the case of Frater 132 you will see that it would not be specifically correct to call it a "Magickal Child" in his working but we can call it a "magickal psychic force." You will also note that it would not be necessary to guard his "magickal instrument" from other men.

In Los Angeles, Frater 132 started an O.T.O. Lodge with only eight members and his objective was to increase the membership. Here is how he worked. When visitors came to see the performance of the Gnostic Mass he would have sexual union with as many different women visitors as possible, concentrating on the idea that he would "inject" into them a psychic force of attraction to the O.T.O. Also, he dedicated his special paramour partner member to be a "transmitter" of the same psychic force with prospective men with whom she would unite sexually. The testimony that this "worked" very successfully is that within one year there were eighty-five loyal working members.

Then came the time that the woman died and also that the headship of the lodge was turned over to Frater Jopan∴. Frater 132 married a woman who was dedicated to the transcendental attainment of Frater 132 himself. She thereby became his exclusive magickal instrument with whom he confined his Sex Magick for the generation of the actual Magickal Child to aid, guard, and to help in attaining spiritual transcendence. The testimony of the result is that I personally testify that Frater 132 attained to the "Knowledge and Conversation" of that "God" incarnate within him—and his wife also attained much.

A digression. As previously stated, the secrets of the Templar Sex Magick have been closely guarded for centuries and have never (previous to my publication of *The Complete Magick Curriculum of the Secret Order G∴B∴G∴*) been clearly revealed in print. I was given a special dispensation to reveal these secrets in print for the first time but under the command of only when I was ready to "assume all responsibility." To me, this "responsibility" means that I take the flatfooted stand that *all Sex Magick* should be dedicated to the attainment of the Knowledge and Conversation of one Daemon which is to say, dedicated to the Great Work which is spiritual transcendence. This is to say also most definitely that such should be the nature of the Magickal Child. True, the Magickal Child may be of a nature to aid one, for example in divination or ESP, but insomuch as this may be an aid and illumination in the attainment of the Great Work. Nor do I deny that success in some materialistic endeavor may also be an aid in following the Great Work.

To continue with the digression concerning when *not* to resort to Magick, Crowley wrote several times and very clearly, "When one desires material things and one can get them by material methods it is a violation of spiritual law" that one resort to Magick to get the desired results. In other words, do not commit the inexcusable thing of "mixing the planes," but keep material things on the material plane and spiritual things on the spiritual plane—a great part of my "responsibility." For me, full "responsibility" means to present the contents of this manual in such a manner as to attract the interest of almost all of those who will see that it is legitimate high Magick in the Great Work and that it should never be debased for selfish, materialistic desires, and also that the publisher is of the same dedication and has an outlet for those sincerely interested in self-transcendence.

This digression is closed with the reminder to the reader that I do not write from theory. I have had charge of about twenty people, men and women, practicing Sex Magick. I know their experiences and records intimately, and nothing can compare with personal experience which should throw theory alone into limbo. Therefore case histories of personal practices and experiences must rightfully take precedence.

Case history: In this kind of case, the emotions and feelings (and even the character of the operators) are so deeply involved that too much of it is lost in giving a secondhand report. For this reason, I, the author, must resort to using an account which is my own experience, and I do so unwillingly.

On very short acquaintance I met and married a native Mexican woman. It so happened that she had certain obligations on the Mexican side of the border and could visit me in the States only on weekends. This we did on six weekends before she left on a trip to the ranch of her father, some distance into Mexico. For convenience and also for sentimental reasons, I gave my wife, whose real name was Pachita, a pet name for Francisca.

Pachita was very honest and sincere in her relationship with me (always a great advantage) and she told me that she could never love me, saying, "It is my nature. My heart is as hard as a rock and I can never really love any man." By this she meant that she could not even treat me with affection and this is almost equivalent to having three strikes against one—but not quite so. The saving grace was that she was very ardent in sexual union with me. Now this is an important point. Although it may seem to be a hopeless case with the intended magickal partner, nevertheless if there is sufficient rapport so that the woman will be ardent with her partner, then there is a good, hopeful promise. All readers should consider the well-established observation that there should be something that is in one's favor for a good operation in Sex Magick. According to my experience and the observance of others, there should be at least enough rapport between the two partners so that there can be some ardent affection during the sexual congrex. Without this it may be almost hopeless for an ideal result in the objective of a Magickal Offspring.

To repeat: with Pachita there was at least an ardent affection during the sexual congrex—and quite willingly given. There is magick in the sexual union in its own self! Although Pachita would never permit me to kiss and caress her when we were not in bed, nevertheless the reader can see how different she was in bed. Yes, there is magick in the sex act—and even both ways—on the one hand idealistically and inspirationally or on the other hand, degrading and taken down into the gutter. Consider this well.

Eight different nights I was in union with Pachita, practicing the grade of Sex Magick for begetting a Magickal Offspring, of which she knew nothing, nor was she consciously aware of anything unusual, although she was undoubtedly, unconsciously, aware of something unusual. In conformity with what I have already written, I dampened down my awareness and consciousness of her as the ordinary personality of Pachita. Instead, in my magickal imagination, she was no less than a goddess, more than Isis, in fact, the embodiment of her Holy∴Guardian∴Angel∴. And more than this: she was also a pyschical manifestation of my H∴G∴A∴. The nature of the Magickal Child was magickally willed to be an autonomous force of both physical and transcendental love. As each congrex followed I noticed that she became more ardent in sexual union and more desirous of prolonging the time of the union instead of immediately "lusting for result." As is written in *The Book of the Law:* "For pure will, unassuaged of purpose, delivered from the lust of result, is every way perfect."

Then came the day for her to leave for the ranch in Mexico. For the first time, in her day clothes, she embraced and kissed me, saying: "I told you that I could never love you and now suddenly I find that I love you in a way that I thought nobody could love. I take a part of you with me and I leave a part of myself with you also. If I die before you I will not be jealous if another woman is in your arms because then also I will be in your arms—the real one that is in your arms: and so it will be with me also if you die first, the real you will be in my arms."

It is written in *The Book of the Law:* "I am above you and in you. My ecstasy is in yours. My joy is to see your joy. . . . The winged globe, the starry blue, are mine, O Ankh-af-na-khonsu!" And with what seemed to be an unconscious premonition she added, "I will be a diamond in the sky forever for your eyes." Yes, she died in an automobile accident in Mexico.

By whatever force and how, who knows, I knew the day and the hour that she was sending the message to me to look into the sky for that diamond. She had left with a part of me and I was a walking zombie for three months. That was three years ago and I cannot bring myself to have union with a woman who is not worthy of being an embodiment of her love, with whom I can think and feel, "I, Pachita, also am with you."

In this chapter I am giving many ways that the Magickal Child or transferred psychic force may manifest. In this case history the reader can see one of several different cases where the Magickal Offspring attaches to the sexual partner—if so directed by the man.

In conclusion on this particular case I admit that it has not been easy to let my hair down and reveal my own feelings in such an intimate manner. Already in telling a friend of mine, who is a psychologist, about this experience, he came back at me with the cutting comment, "You are an expert in *self-deception*." Naturally he means my "crazy imagination." Yet he knows very well that the very foundation of all Magick worthy of notice is the *magickal imagination.* If any reader is inclined toward the belief that the *Magickal Imagination is self-deception,* then that reader should not assay magickal practices or it will indeed be a real self-deception.

This next case is about a cat and a dog being the focus for the Magickal Offspring. Mrs. M.P. and a carpenter friend were put to the task of building a thirteen-hundred-square-foot house that had to be built in accordance with a rigid building code and yet cost no more than two-thirds of what a contractor would charge. So the two of them set to doing all of the work themselves with the exception of the plumbing and the electrical work. From the very outset they ran into unforeseen and unfortunate problems. To cut the story short, the two of them performed the sex magick rituals, using the unique method of directing the creation to be embodied (or carried by) the cat and the dog.

Strangely enough, the cat developed a rare curiosity streak. Typically, it often would put its paw on the particular thing that they were working on. One example is enough, as follows. They saw the cat put its paw on a plumbing outlet which had been done by the plumber. Thereupon it was discovered that the outlet had not been installed in the proper place. By discovering this and correcting it then, they saved about $400. Such things happened about six times with their cat. I do not mean to imply that every time the cat put its paw on the work that it helped us. What was actually happening was that we were brought to a point of acute awareness in recognizing the "message" when it had some real application. It was the cat's method and would be much the same as when a person talks. We would not recognize help on the house if a person was talking about a fish that he had caught, but, on the other hand, we would be aware enough if he started to talk about something worth considering.

One account of Bobbie the dog's actions is enough. The workers had gone to town and no one was at the building project. The hay barn and horse stable had caught fire. Bobbie ran to a neighbor's house, barking, even hurling himself against the plate glass door to get attention. By that time, the neighbors saw that it was burning furiously but they came to the fire anyway. Typical of horses in a fire, they know of only one refuge when they panic. They go into a sort of hysterical trauma and stand huddled together in the burning building. Bobbie went into the blazing building and had to fight the horse to force it out of the blaze. The cat also had kittens in the building and it ran in to save her kittens. Bobbie ran into the blazing building and brought the cat out in his teeth. Two times more the cat ran into the building and two times more Bobbie dashed into the blaze and brought her out in his teeth. By that time almost all of their fur had been singed away and it was several days before they could stand on their burned feet. Mrs. M.P. had a purchaser for her high-bred horse at $600 and she desperately needed this money to finish the house. Bobbie had saved the day—and the magick cat!

Case history of the Grand Experiment. I decided to get a number of people to practice Sex Magick under my direction in order to get definite evidence on results by the proof from a number of different people. In selecting these people they had to all come up to what I regard as standard requirements for good or successful results. One does not expect a person to be capable of surveying if he cannot even calculate simple arithmetic, much less geometry and trigonometry.

Here follows a list of the requirements that I demanded:

(1) That they still have the potential and capacity for what Crowley has called energized enthusiasm. This implies that the man (or woman) is capable of something more than the physical release of an itch between the legs, which also implies that the person is at least potentially capable of the inspiration of the union of two souls—something spiritually or psychically.

(2) Some people find it easy to make or feel a rapport with many other people and upon relatively short acquaintance. This ranges on down to people who find it difficult to establish a rapport with even only one or two other persons. This rapport gives very great help in complying with other conditions: in the magickal congrex being a must.

(3) A few simple questions were usually enough for me to determine if a person was incapable of having any ability in making the imagination subjectively real. This ranges from no ability or desire for imagination on up to those with an active and inspired imagination. Some ability in invoking and evoking the imagination is a must in all magick workings, particularly to a point of subjective reality. *In my book* A Manual of Psychic Self-Defense, *(forthcoming from Llewellyn Publications) Dr. Stefen Hoeller has written an extensive and most valuable treatise on the subject of reality, subjective and objective. Everyone seriously concerned with*

*occultism, psychology and Magick should read this
article.*

But how to get a number of suitable people for the
experiment? I had a wonderful opportunity. In those days of
the early forties (even the late thirties) it was the custom of
the O.T.O. to throw a big party every three months. They
called it the "Crowley Party" because all of the entrance fee
monies was sent to Crowley. On the occasion of this
particular party, it was to be followed by another grand
party only two weeks later. These two parties were attended
by 300 people: discounting the fifty repeaters, 150 different
people attended, but all of them had some interest in
metaphysics, occultism or Magick. This ranged from those
with serious interest on down to the dilettantes and those
just seeing something—something which they knew not.

After diligent selection I gave three lectures of
instructions to twice as many people as I had hoped to
have. Some of them volunteered to pull out on the
grounds that they did not have what it takes. One man
said, "I should blot out my awareness that it is my wife? I
could easily imagine that she is a favorite daughter of old
Nick and we could do some great Black Magick." His wife
responded with, "I could easily imagine most any man to
be a gift of the gods to me but he would not let me. He
would want to make sure that I was as ready as ever *for
him* to pounce me every night."

Then I gave them two weeks to go through the working
of the Second Degree, Dianism, for no less than two times
and preferably more. They were then ready to show me
the record of their experiences, from their weakest points
to their strongest points. The purpose of this was to cut
down the number of people still more. Another two weeks
was given and I wound up with eight partners, very close
to the number that I had hoped to have. I then gave them

two months more to practice Dianism, requiring each one to give me a record every week.

At the end of the two-month practice, I had very good reports from all of them. They were proving the validity of my contention: (1) That Dianism can be practiced very frequently without losing one's desire and virility for the working; (2) That if performed correctly and with sufficient inspired imagination, it brings spiritual transcendence.

As I see it, there is no need to resort to the Third Degree, Quodosch, except for very special occasions. I leave those who are ready to decide just where and when those special occasions are the best for the Great Work.

The sixth month saw the termination of the experiment. I again went over all the records that they had submitted to me monthly and also had a long conversation with each of the performers (eight men and eight women). The following is my honest and studied determination of the advancement of each one of the sixteen, but first I must explain the meaning or significance of the four spheres on the Tree of Life which are being used for describing the "grades."

Tiphareth to which is attached the description of "brilliance" and the Sun. This is the grade or sphere ruling the Knowledge and Conversation of the Holy Guardian Angel—one's Daemon. (Note: actual *union* with the H∴G∴A∴ is of a higher sphere.)

The next sphere below Tiphareth is Netzach—Venus and Beauty. The next one below is Hod, Splendor, Mercury, Inspired Mind.

Below Hod is Yesod—the Moon, refined emotions. The next below is the lowest, Malkuth, the physical universe.

My determination: There were two who attained to Tiphareth of Tiphareth—autonomous Knowledge and Conversation of one's Daemon (the H∴G∴A∴); two who attained to Tiphareth of Netzach—attainment to the Knowledge and Conversation of the H∴G∴A∴ on the plane of Venus—Growth, Love and Beauty; four who attained to Tiphareth of Hod, which is on the plane of inspired mind and intellect.

Then there were clearly four who had unquestionably attained to Tiphareth of Yesod, implying that the Knowledge and Conversation of the H∴G∴A∴ is limited to the feelings and emotions, a sort of emotional enchantment.

The lowest four had not reached Tiphareth on any plane *but* the emotions and feelings had been brought to a higher plane than the ordinary. I characterized this as Yesod of Yesod. Prosper chance, I describe it as soulful enchantment and closer to Mother Nature even as little children under the age of six, but with much more *awareness.*

Here is what will be very incredible to practically all readers concerning these results of the six months of practice in Dianism. In analyzing it percentage wise, it clearly proves that it far surpasses other methods of magickal practice for self-transcendence. And this was accomplished with only the Second Degree, Dianism, while the Third Degree, Quodosch, is still more potent and efficient. It will be so ridiculous and unbelievable to all those who have read many books of "High Authority" which extol other methods (and no mention of Sex Magick) that I have neither hope nor expectations that more than 5 percent of all readers of this book will "believe" it.

There will also be some die-hard quibblers who will say that I screened out the best people for the experiment but this is not really so. This speciality is the rule in whatever one wishes to specialize in, in the occult and magick field. For example, only those who have a talent or liking for reasoning by the art of "synthesis" should study astrology (or submit to an experiment). A person may be ever so gifted in the field of Magick but if his mind and general psychology be not in rapport with the Tarot cards as a method of divination, then all sixteen of them would flunk in a test of accomplishment in it.

It is equally a fact that people should have what we might call a normally satisfactory sexual life and makeup for assaying practice in Sex Magick, plus some ability in the use of the magickal imagination. In fact, any person who cannot invoke and evoke the magickal imagination is clearly *off base* in performing any magickal practice and, without doubt, that is why there are ten readers of Magick for every one who holds magickal practices!

Back to the experimenters after the foregoing digression. I gave them some instructions and explanations of the Third Degree, Quodosch. I told them that I was limiting the instructions to the methods of making the partner become the "magickal instrument"—but more: that the partner be made the physical presence or embodiment of one's H∴G∴A∴, but *more than this,* which is that the partner is regarded as the embodiment of the Magickal Offspring.

One of those who had attained to Tiphareth protested, "But you have already instructed us to attain to this by the Second Degree, Dianism method."

I explained that they would see several differences after some practice: also that it would be an *autonomous* force and would operate automatically even when not asked to—and more powerfully.

I gave a few pointers such as would operate both as a mnemonics but would also give more living strength to the Magickal Offspring by the following methods:

(1) To use a special bed sheet for the congrex and magickal orisons which was not to be frequently washed.

(2) To have a special place for a kiss for the magickal partner which might be on the forehead at the approximate locality of the pineal gland or on the mouth or any other suitable place whatsoever on the body.

I also gave them a method concerning making a letter very powerful to accomplish the intended result (as given previously in this manual). But first one should also have a "pantacle" which is a special design which you have conceived and drawn which is a symbol of your particular magickal aspiration (including also your own character and magickal nature insofar as you can divine it). One should habitually "anoint" this pantacle regularly with the "essence" to give and continue its strength. You are then in good practice for the method of treating your letter. Anoint the sheet of writing paper with a few spots. Allow it to dry for a few minutes and then write your letter on this sheet. By this method your mental process is at its best and you will write a better letter than you ordinarily would write. Seal it in the envelope as soon as it is finished.

I know of one case where the recipient was moved to respond to such a letter in exactly the opposite way from what he had intended to write. It caused the recipient of the letter to give the job to the writer despite the fact that he had already decided to give it to another person. He said, "I don't know why I sent for you; I wanted to give the job to Doc. Wallace." But such things can "boomerang" to one's discomfort—and it did! He made things very unpleasant and finally too difficult for the person that he had hired. Take care: let it not be a case that can boomerang. He, the boss, continually and heatedly complained, "I don't know why in hell I hired you when I wanted to hire somebody else. What in the devil are you? Some kind of a witch?"

This chapter should contain also an account of the Reformed Order of the Palladians, founded in France before the turn of the century. Before this there was a Palladian Order in Italy which was one of the many side orders of Freemasonry. Some of them were even comasonry. With quite a fanfare it was announced that a lineal descendent of the celebrated mystic and occultist Thomas Vaughan of England had been discovered in Paris and that she was a woman of the highest magickal attainment. It was not long before a substantial membership had been taken in the Order.

The head propaganda man in this was a French writer named Leo Taxil (his pen name) and there was also a German occultist, Sachs, with the pen name of Dr. Bataille. Both had been Catholics but finally "defected" and were Freemasons.

Leo Taxil put out many writings to the public press about this Order of Palladians. I have never been able to discover why this "supposed" movement incurred so much hostility from both the Church and the government; both of them were out for blood.

Here is the account of the Palladians of Leo Taxil that one will read in the British and American encyclopedias, various magazine articles and two paperbacks. No one had seen the notorious Diana Vaughn and people were demanding that they see her and also for other proof of Taxil's "veracity." Then came the time when Taxil could not evade these demands any longer. He named the day, time, and place when he would appear with Diana Vaughn and with other evidence. A great crowd awaited him. He unabashedly stated that he had hoaxed everybody and that Diana Vaughn was nothing but the name of his typewriter. What one reads is that it was nothing but a great hoax by Taxil.

Now for the other side of the story. Mrs. Nestor Webster, in her book *Secret Societies and Subversive Movements,* does not call it a hoax and writes on it for real: likewise does the Catholic encyclopedia. There is definite proof that one of the three founders of the Hermetic Order of the Golden Dawn, Dr. Westcott, was associated with the Order and he certainly was not the kind of man to be an active party in perpetuating a hoax.

It so happens that my good friend Clarke Walker was in France in the early part of 1894. He was always interested in anything in throes of a lively beginning and particularly in the occult. From what he found out about this Palladian movement he became intrigued enough to apply for a United States Charter of the Palladian Order and he told me that he paid $2,000 for this charter. A photocopy of this charter and also a copy of his turning the charter over to me are reproduced on the following pages. Note that it is dated the 13th day of January, 1894. Also note that Diana Vaughn and Dr. Westcott are signers of this charter. Note also that on the first day of January, 1938, he turned the charter over to me. It is well to add that Clarke Walker was not the kind of gullible mark to have been hoaxed in the manner that is publically recounted.

Walker was informed that there was just one grand secret of the Order which was that there be a connecting link between some "initiated" member and any and all succeeding members, which was told to him as follows. Diana Vaughn as the Central Force of the "dispensation" had held sexual union with Dr. Battaille and Dr. Westcott. These men in turn would "initiate" women members in like manner and then these women would initiate new-coming men in like manner forming a continuous hierarchical chain. Because of the special charter for the United States, Clarke informed me that he had been "initiated" by none other than Diana Vaughn herself.

I, Clarke A. Walker, Supreme Grand
Commander of Ordo Palladium Reformado
do hereby grant unto Louis T. Culling
my supreme authority in this Order,
together with all rites and secrets
of Ordo Palladium Reformado.

Signed this

First day of January, 1938

Clarke A. Walker

Ordo Palladium
  Du Europe et du Monde
Par la proclamation de
l' Ordo Palladium +
  Nous accordons
     à
Monseigneur Papus Clarke Walker
la charte d' authorité
suprême de l' Ordo
Palladium pour et dans
les États-Unis de
l' Amerique
13 I I 1894

GRA∴ INSP *Diana Vaughn*

GR∴ CHANC. *Dr. Bataille∴*

GR∴ SEC. *Leo Taxil*

GR∴ COMM. *Dr. W. Westcott*

Clarke "initiated" the wife of a noted writer in this country and she, in turn, did likewise with me. I was astounded to see the great force that this chain-link method had generated. It was very powerful. It was not long after Clarke's arrival to the States and his initiation of the person previously mentioned that the news came out about the great hoax perpetrated by Taxil. Walker then completely gave up the idea of doing anything with the charter. When he turned the charter over to me he said "I have the feeling that you can use it to some good purpose." That purpose has been served by using it as a case history and to testify to the magickal potency of the "link-chain sex" method. So ends this subject except to state that all members of the past have reached the age of death and that I am the sole living member.

It is impossible to disassociate the name of Aleister Crowley, the Great Beast 666, from Sex Magick. If one takes the two books on Crowley by Symonds as completely authentic then it would and could steer many people askance from all Sex Magick, no matter on how high a plane its presentation may be. Therefore, I think that this book would be lacking if it did not have a word to say about A.C. (as he was often called by his followers).

Was he some kind of crude sensual sex fiend as Symonds has represented him to be? There are some important verses in one of Crowley's poems called "Divine Synthesis." One should read it and read it more than once to see a Crowley that is the opposite of the picture that Symonds has painted. The very humanness, its depth of soul appeal chokes me up and brings tears to my eyes. It shows a Crowley that such a low bastard as Symonds could never possibly see or understand. In Israel Regardie's book *The Best of Crowley*, (forthcoming from Llewellyn Publications) one can get a far different picture of Crowley. Then to top it all, there is Regardie's *The Eye in the Triangle* (St. Paul: Llewellyn Publications, 1970) about Crowley. In this book, if one sees the devil in Crowley then one is also forced to see a great spiritual soul. We are also forced to see the same in ourselves.

Let us not forget the high character and great result of the Sex Magick between Crowley and his wife Rose. He used her as his magickal instrument with great sincerity and he made of her his great Magickal Offspring. It was, as a consequence, she who led him to the magick Stele of Revealing. It was she who gave the methods for the ritual of the great "revealing" which finally resulted in Crowley's becoming the "instrument" for giving forth *The Book of the Law*. Rose was actually the informer and director of Crowley's own H∴G∴A∴, operating autonomously in her body. Indeed, she, Rose, was the embodiment of not only his Magickal Offspring but also the psychical embodiment of Crowley's own Daemon.

For the information of those who are seeking all possible knowledge pertinent to Sex Magick, it must be here stated that *The Book of the Law* is loaded with pointers on Sex Magick from the beginning to the end of the book.

For those who have no access to *The Book of the Law,* they can find the first of the three chapters in my book *The Complete Magick Curriculum of the Secret Order G∴B∴G∴,* beginning on page 53. It also contains relevant commentaries to each verse written by Crowley. But enough of Crowley.

I believe that most every man and woman senses a lack in himself or herself—not being "complete." It may well be that what they feel is their unconsciousness of their "other self." Sexual union fulfills this desire for completeness, at least in most people, and can therefore be a medicine for the soul. But for those who would decry

Sex Magick as something evil or degrading it can be answered that they are denigrating that which is far more spiritual than their own habitual congrex, even if not carried to the point of assiduously following the way of transcendental Sex Magick. The "ordinary" way is *invita Minerva*—lacking inspiration.

APPENDICES

DAMIANA: THE PSYCHIC APHRODISIAC

I give you fair warning: this article asserts that there is a certain medicine, Damiana, which has an astounding communicative effect upon certain people when they are in association with that person who has taken the medicine.

But hold on! This is not the lucubration of a disordered intellect. There has been no contact with the little green people from Mars. In fact, the testimonies of personal experience are from people who are well trained in the art of critical observation, including myself.

As briefly as possible, here are the dry, technical details. Damiana is a plant native to Mexico. The dried leaves can be purchased for a local or a mail-order dealer in herbs. The dosage and regimen used for our case histories is an follows: two heaping tablespoons of the leaves to one large cup of water. Boil slowly for five minutes; allow to stand until cool and drain the liquid. Drink this liquid in the evening; continue for two weeks.

As a preliminary to presenting the case history of my own experience with Damiana, I want to explain the format of this account. In a case like this, one does not take chances with the vagaries of memory; therefore, the record was written as a sort of diary while I was involved in the actual experience.

Record of C. T. L., age 69, 1962

October 7. Start two week regimen of Damiana.

October 17. Women between 35 and 45 years of age, who in the past have regarded me as beyond their age group, suddenly seem to be interested in me. Is this my imagination?

October 21. The idea of having a woman in my arms is a delightful picture. Speaking some Spanish, and having a penchant for Mexican chiquitas, I leave Los Angeles for Tijuana, Mexico.

October 21 continued. Become friendly with a waitress in a restaurant in Tijuana, a woman of 33 years of age and of singular beauty. Ordinarily, she should not have given a second look to a man of my age and appearance. She has agreed to come to my room at the end of her afternoon shift, at 3:00 P.M. I am feeling more certain that there is some kind of magic in this Damiana, and I have fortified myself with a pint of Damiana Liqueur, which one can buy in Mexico.

3:30 to 5:00 P.M. United in love. She both gave and received amorously and even affectionately. After her night shift, ending at 9:00 P.M., she is going to return "sonar toda la noche contigo"—to dream the whole night with me.

October 22, 9:00 A.M. Last night was like being in an Arabian Night's story. Four times was La Encantadora taken on the magic carpet to the mountain of ecstasy. Three times I sailed with her—already an incredible exploit for me. Yet she has said that she is going to be with me again the coming afternoon and night! It is time for that feeling of complete surfeit. Yet I am looking forward to this with an enchanted imagination that rivals the anticipation of the first love affair of my youth.

I have taken her to her restaurant. Three waitresses have crowded around us saying, "What has this Americano done with you? Such stars in your eyes!" I am now almost certain that there is something that is communicative about this Damiana. I am going down to the herbalist to get some; the liqueur does not have sufficient medicinal strength.

October 23, 11:00 A.M. Last night was a night of love's enchantment, even greater than the previous night. When we awakened late this morning, it should have been (by past experience) the time when there is too much of a muchness, and the mere idea of love play is unwelcome. But such is not the case. Her breath is still perfume. There is no criticism of her personality that is possible. I can see nothing in her but sexual perfection. Again, when I went with her to the restaurant, the waitresses gathered around in wonderment—two afternoons and two nights and still stars in the eyes!

Upon arriving back to Los Angeles I saw a Mexican woman in a taco and beer joint. I was still in the mood for love play. She appeared to be half-crocked and my opening gambit was to buy kisses from her at twenty-five cents per kiss. After spending almost two dollars in this manner she suddenly wilted and tried to go to sleep on my shoulder.

Now the experience of one person is not entirely convincing, but there were three other men and one woman who had also made the Damiana test for this record. The three men also had experiences which paralleled my experience. While not so extended and intense as in my case, they did have convincing evidence of this phenomenon which I call *communicative*.

The record of the woman was even more outstanding than my own record, particularly the communicative aspect.

All of us then agreed to extend the experiment for another two weeks, but without any sexual play. Again their experience was in convincing agreement with my own experience. We noticed, in particular, that people who would ordinarily have conversed with us quite casually were unusually friendly, even to the point of intimate interest.

At the time that this period was closing I met a woman who was not many years past being half my age—beautiful but of a reserved nature; however, she soon warmed up in talking with me. She told me that very few men could attract her sexually and therefore she had been involved in very few love escapades.

Within the hour she had asked me to take a weekend trip with her, in her car and as her guest.

She had told me the truth. She was out of practice, but thanks to Damiana, instinct, and intuition, her warm blood was soon in full possession of her.

In conclusion, it must be stated that my associates and I are fully aware of the various psychological factors which can be involved when one follows such a regimen as our Damiana experiment. There is the faith in medicines and magic fetishes, which in turn can bring about an added confidence (and even a potent imagination) which may produce some remarkable psychological results. We have given this its due consideration, and have duly discounted it.

The administrator of the Los Angeles office of the California Food and Drug Administration has said to me that it is his opinion that all so-called aphrodisiacs are merely psychological in result. We certainly cannot agree with him, in this case.

Our experience is that Damiana is a very effective and healthful tonic for the sexual system. Of course, it is axiomatic that sexual virility is conducive to the imagination of things sexual.

Our experiments show conclusively that there is something that is sexually attractive, that is communicative, that emanates from the subject who has taken Damiana for an adequate period of time. We do not pretend to solve the mechanism behind this phenomenon, but the very foundation of the scientific method is to give due consideration to the results of empirical experiments. They are not to be denied.

APPENDIX II

MARIJUANA AND CHAMPAGNE

Probably the most difficult part of the whole magickal operation is the required attitude toward the woman partner, in which the man should lose all possible awareness that she is a definite personality that he knows, even to erasing her name. The requirement is that you identify her as a goddess in manifestation, and better yet, that she becomes the embodiment of one's own Daemon—one's Heavenly Lover.

Surely you can see how it would be impossible to kid yourself that the red ruby gem in your ring is a green garnet, unless you can temporarily erase your awareness that it is a ruby.

For the first three months I found it impossible to remove from my persisting consciousness that my partner was my wife with all her characteristics. How to overcome this persisting indentification? It seemed impossible for me.

I had read that Marijuana had one characteristic that was uniquely different from all other drugs of hallucinatory nature: that the result from Marijuana would conform to one's predetermined, desired emotion or imagination. If one concentrates on having the mind taken down into the gutter, that is where it will take one. Equally so will the willed imagination, with Marijuana, takes one to an enchanted heavenly land. For that good reason I decided to test it.

I smoked the cigarette while we were lying in bed. I did not attempt any negation, such as trying to forget that she was my wife, but instead of this I directed my imagination to see that she was becoming like a goddess and I began to feel it, i.e., the imagination was becoming subjectively real, rapidly and without strain.

Due to previous practices, I was amost led automatically into the next step in which she was the embodied presence of my own Divine Lover—the Holy Guardian Angel, the Daemon, the most sublime loving presence.

The ice was broken with only one marijuana cigarette! From the time on it was ever so much easier and faster to bring the aspiration to subjective reality, and a subjective reality that engendered no small amount of objective reality.

Throughout the United States there were 79 initiate members taking part in this Magick in a secret order. Assuming that these members would like to find some help in attaining faster success in this congrex rite, I suggested to headquarters that they test the following two aids: (1) champagne and (2) damiana tea. (Because Marijuana is severely against the law, it was not to be tested in this case.)

Champagne must be taken by both parties, and it must be very cold. The whole bottle (one-fifth of a gallon) should be taken fairly fast, rather than sipping slowly.

The Damiana was taken as follows: beginning on the morning of the day before the congrex, a large dose of the brewed tea was taken, continuing every four hours with the same until the time of the congrex.

After testing, 27 reported good success with champagne; 23 reported success with Damiana. Note that success with Damiana was not as strong as with champagne. This is because the Damiana tea regimen should begin three days previous to the congrex.

In explaining the action of champagne, please understand that there is no other wine substitute which is satisfactory. Champagne has a very low alcoholic content (a higher content is not required) but there is a special way it works. When it is very cold, it causes the flap in the stomach leading to the bowels to close. After the stomach warms the liquid, in conjunction with the carbonic gas charge, the flap opens up and the entire quantity of liquid is dumped at once into the next bowel section. The result is that it acts quite differently from other alcoholic beverages.

The main difficulty with Damiana is that it is not carried in small herbal stores although larger stores (and mail-order houses) usually do carry it.

Later it was discovered that the use of a certain capsule is effective. In this capsule are equal parts of the downers and the uppers i.e., tranquilizer and stimulator. Doctors sometimes prescribe this for weight reduction, often under the trade name of Dexamil. A doctor's prescription is required to purchase these capsules. There are objections to their use and I cannot conscientiously recommend their usage.

Some magickal success has been achieved by using a very simple vegetable juice that will surprise you. Drink one pint of raw beet juice about twenty minutes before expecting a result. Then be surprised! Remember, not less than one pint.

And do not forget the effectiveness of the practice of the First Degree, Alphaism, when properly and consistently practiced.

SUFI PHILOSOPHY

Sufism is well defined in the dictionary as a system and practice of mysticism (and Magick) developed especially in Persia into an elaborate symbolic system much used by their poets.

In fact, there is very little adequately written, even in Arabic, in plain language. The Sufi poets date from the ninth century up to the time of the Sufi poet, best known in this country for his *Rubaiyat,* Omar Khayyam, circa 1123 A.D.

About the translation of the *Rubaiyat* by Fitzgerald, a high Sufi says, "Fitzgerald, in spite of himself, was permeated with Sufistic ideas and his translation shows how he was filled with Omar's spirit." Therefore, the tranlation by Fitzgerald is adequate; however, the import of the symbolism is dark to the reader without adequate explanatory notes by a high Sufi. For this reason the commentary is appended to the poetry which is included in this book.

The Sufi commentator writes, "Besides writing the commentary notes, we have also endeavored to retouch a few lines that they may stand out more distinctly. In the name of Al-Ahad."

Only those portions of the *Rubaiyat* which apply to Sex Magick are given herein. It is given in this text as having great magickal value by itself. Here is the magick: if the aspirant reads these lines from the *Rubaiyat* on several occasions, he will attain, as if by magic, a great amount of inspiration in the practice of the ecstatic congrex. In the same manner do religious people gain great spiritual inspiration when reading certain parts of the "Song of Solomon" from the Bible, or from listening to the music, "Elizabet's Prayer" by Wagner.

Inspiration is a precious thing to invoke and there is no doubt that when these verses are understood there will result much added inspiration. It is for this reason that these verses and the commentary are included in this book, albeit it also shows clearly the source fountain of Western Sex Magick.

Thus sang Fitzgerald:

4

Now the New Year reviving old Desires,
The thoughtful Soul to Solitude retires,
Where the White Hand of Moses on the Bough
Puts out, and Jesus from the ground suspires.

5

Tram indeed is gone with all his Rose
And Jamshyd's Sev'n-ring'd Cup where no one knows;
But still a Ruby kindles in the Vine,
And many a Garden by the Water blows.

6

And David's lips are lock't; but in divine
High-piping Pehlevi, with "Wine! Wine! Wine!
Red Wine!"—the Nightingale cries to the Rose
That Sallow cheek of hers t'incarnadine.

Thus spake Omar, the Sufi:

... Let Tram and Jamshyd's cup be gone! Of small concern is it that David sings no more. Love, the Everlasting, is red as wine, strong as wine, and gives wisdom as does wine! "Come, fill the cup!" Be young and fling away the old garments; there is but a little time to realize the preciousness of the Holy One and the Presence of Al-Aziz, the Incomparable, who is also Wadud, the All-Loving!

"If it appear to have a brim, 'tis the fault of the cup."

The Sufi is no wine-bibber and the poet is no drunkard. The Sufi calls:

"... bring me a cup of wine!
Not wine that drives away wisdom,
But that unmixed wine whose hidden power
*   vanquishes Fate;*
That clear wine with which the worshipper sanctifies
*   the garb of the heart;*
That illuminating wine which shows lovers of the
*   world the true path;*
That impearling wine which cleanses the meditative
*   mind of fanciful thoughts."*

It was but a trifle that brought wine in disrespect:

"Allah hath promised wine in Paradise,
Why then should wine on earth be deemed a vice?
An Arab in his cups cut Hamzah's girth,—
For that sole cause was drink declared a vice."

In this case, wine is the inspiration of sex magick love directed to one's own Daemon—one's Divine Lover.

Thus sang Fitzgerald:

7

> *Come, fill the Cup, and in the fire of Spring*
> *Your Winter garment of Repentance fling:*
> *The Bird of Time has but a little way*
> *To flutter—and the Bird is on the Wing.*

8

> *Whether at Naishapur or Babylon,*
> *Whether the Cup with sweet or bitter run,*
> *The Wine of Life keeps oozing drop by drop,*
> *The Leaves of Life keep falling one by one.*

Thus spake Omar, the Sufi:

> *"Life's fount is wine, Khizr its guardian,*
> *I, like Elias, find it where I can;*
> *'Tis sustenance for heart and spirit too,*
> *Allah himself calls wine 'a boon to man.' "*

The Sufi scorns material essences: the wine he drinks is wisdom from the vats of Allah, "the Eternal Saki." Therefore, says the Sufi:

> *"Where have I said that wine is wrong for all?*
> *'Tis lawful for the wise, but not for fools."*

Wisdom is the law for the wise, but not for fools. How could it be? Foolishness knows not wisdom. Learn from the Sufi that

> *"Cup is the body, and soul is the wine."*

The *cup* is not only the physical body, it is also that of the woman partner, becoming a sacred cup.

Thus sang Fitzgerald:

9

Each Morn a thousand Roses brings, you say;
Yes, but where leaves the Rose of Yesterday?
And this first Summer month that brings the Rose
Shall the Jamshyd and Kaikobad away.

10

Well, let it take them! What have we to do
With Kaikobad the Great, or Kaikhosru?
Let Zal and Rustum bluster as they will,
Or Hatim call to Supper—heed not you.

Thus spake Omar, the Sufi:

. . . Wine is that ocean in which sails the ship divine, called Love. An emblem of that caravel is the rose. In the world there are two kinds of roses: one that comes in the spring and leaves before summer. The nightingale will stay with that rose as long as he may, till in amorous intoxication he at last falls down "where thorns point their daggers at his bleeding breast." The Sufi, too, loves this rose; still, he will say with the caviller: "Where leaves the rose of yesterday?" He knows, however, that the rose of yesterday is the rose of to-day in transmutation. The Eternal Womb is never barren. There is another rose: a rose of mystery. Its petals are the planetary curves, and its stamens and pistils are Divine Presences. The Sufi reveres that rose. In it he finds the Beloved.

The *rose* is also the woman partner when she, by the magickal imagination, is *transmuted* to become the objective manifestation of the Divine Daemon.

Thus sang Fitzgerald:

12

A Book of Verses underneath the Bough,
A Jug of Wine, a Loaf of Bread—and Thou
Beside me singing in the Wilderness—
Oh, Wilderness were Paradise enow!

Thus spake Omar, the Sufi:

The Sufi sings of the vanity of the phenomenal world. He retires under the Tuba-tree with a "book of verses," written by the Beloved, his God. The Tuba-tree sends a branch into every believer's home. It is the tree "whose scent is the breath of eternity," and "whose flowers have a soul in every leaf." He takes along with him "wine and bread," or "heaven and earth," as an alchemist has called them, and

   "THOU
  Beside me singing in the wilderness"—
Who art THOU, but the BELOVED?

———————

Who art Thou, but the Beloved? he silently says to the woman partner, for the Divine Lover—the Daemon, she now is, when under the *Tuba-tree*—the couch of Love.

Thus sang Fitzgerald:

19

I sometimes think that never blows so red
The Rose as where some buried Caesar bled;
That every Hyacinth the Garden wears
Dropt in her Lap from some once lovely Head.

20

And this reviving Herb whose tender Green
Fledges the River-Lip on which we lean—
Ah, lean upon it lightly! for who knows
From what once lovely Lip it springs unseen!

21

Ah, my Beloved, fill the Cup that clears
To-day of past Regret and future Fears:
To-morrow!—Why, To-morrow I may be
Myself with Yesterday's Sev'n thousand Years.

Thus spake Omar, the Sufi:

. . . "the World is the image of God." The Sufi lives as a member of a conscious universe, hence he "spills" wine on the ground as an "ancestral" offering; hence the rose "never blows so red as where some buried Caesar bled"; hence his tenderness for what was perhaps a "once lovely lip."

The Sufi is a man of Wholeness (holiness). He "thinks" God's thoughts are revealed in his whole nature. . . . His will is strong as the ages, and his aspirations are not bound by cycles of eternities. He is equally familiar with "the world of the infinitely small" as that of the larger one. He addresses birds as sisters and reptiles as brothers. He has cleaved an atom and found that it contained a world. There is sympathy or fellow-feeling between him

"And this reviving Herb whose tender Green
Fledges the River-Lip on which we lean—"

The Sufi is a poet, yea, more than a poet. "Tender Greens" and "River-Lips" are symbols and more to him. The curves of Nature's architecture and the eloquence of her colors make his Book. All its lessons are written in volutes of love and straight lines of law. They are imprinted upon leaves of life and illuminated by shafts of light.

Spilling wine upon the ground as an ancestral offering refers to sections of Liber Quodosh in creating the spiritual intelligence and other powers.

Thus sang Fitzgerald:

32

There was the Door to which I found no Key;
There was the Veil through which I might not see:
Some little talk awhile of Me and Thee
There was—and then no more of Thee and Me.

33

Earth could not answer; nor the Seas that mourn
In flowing Purple, of their Lord forlorn;
Nor rolling Heaven, with all his Signs reveal'd
And hidden by the sleeve of Night and Morn.

34

Then of the Thee in Me who works behind
The Veil, I lifted up my hands to find
A Lamp amid the Darkness; and I heard,
As from Without—"The Me within Thee blind!"

Thus spake Omar, the Sufi:

The Sufi speaks of veils which do not hide, but which reveal. The "Me" and the "Thee" are veils through which we do not see. But when there is "no more of Thee and Me," then we see the Mystery in that veil. "Unity" is its Name. In that is unravel'd "the Master-knot of Human Fate" and in that Name we may drink deep and freely. In that Name we read the tablet of Creation. That name is a veil which reveals . . . To be sure the Earth, the Seas, the Heavens cannot answer loudly. Their language is silent, but is nevertheless easily understood by a child. They themselves are the language of the intuitive . . . It is

"The Thee in Me who works behind
The veil."

But to the earth-bound ones it is as mysterious as that of the Universe. . . .

———————

The *Unity* refers to making oneself identify with the Divine Self, the Divine Lover, the Daemon, in the union with the transmuted woman who is identified with the Daemon.

Thus sang Fitzgerald:

39

And not a drop that from our Cups we throw
For Earth to drink of, but may steal below
To quench the fire of Anguish in some Eye
There hidden—far beneath, and long ago.

40

As then the Tulip for her morning sup
Of Heav'nly Vintage from the soil looks up,
Do you devoutly do the like, till Heav'n
To Earth invert you—like an empty Cup.

Thus spake Omar, the Sufi:

. . . Fana is not extinction, but transmutation and ascension. Self-unfoldment is the Sufi's life:

"When you have traveled on from man, you will
*   doubtless become an angel;*
After that you are done with this earth: your station
*   is in Heaven.*
Pass again even from angelhood: enter that Ocean!
Through it all you are and you remain You."

The Sufi while he walks in the garden of the Beloved does, like the Tulip, open his bosom for the "morning sup." In the morning both lift up their eyes to the "Turkis-vaulted dome of the sky" to be united with that Supreme Intelligence that moulded both. When Mother Earth washes the sleep from her eyes with dew and cold breezes, they both "utter speech" and their hearts throb with the One Life of Brotherhood that binds all the spheres in United.

This is the result of sex transmutation described in poetic language.

Thus sang Fitzgerald:

55

You know, my Friends, with what a brave Carouse
I made a Second Marriage in my house;
Divorced old barren Reason from my Bed,
And took the Daughter of the Vine to Spouse.

56

For "Is" and "Is-not" though with Rule and Line,
And "Up-and-down" by Logic I define,
Of all that one should care to fathom, I
Was never deep in anything but—Wine.

Thus spake Omar, the Sufi:

The Sufi never "plays the game of love alone," he is twice-married man. In Youth he takes barren intellect to his bed, but when he tastes "Life's pure elixir," he quickly divorces her for "The Daughter of the Vine." At first by Logic he defines "Is" and "Is-Not." At last he finds the Logos in the Wine—the "trance divine"—for to the Sufi

*"The wine-cup is as Jesus: life once more
Its potent tide can to the dead restore."*

He begins in the Senses, but soon discards them:

"Our senses barren are; they come from barren soil."

He ends in the Heart: " 'the spacious land of God,' 'tis named in Holy Writ.' "

———————

This is the growth from plain sexual love to the inspired sexual congrex with the Divine Lover; the *trance divine.*

Thus sang Fitzgerald:

58

And lately, by the Tavern Door agape,
Came shining through the Dusk an Angel Shape
Bearing a Vessel on his Shoulder; and
He bid me taste of it; and 'twas—the Grape!

59

The Grape that can with Logic absolute
The Two-and-Seventy jarring Sects confute:
The sovereign Alchemist that in a trice
Life's leaden metal into Gold transmute.

Thus spake Omar, the Sufi:

That grape is a veritable alchemist, an "Allah-breathing Lord." Who doubts it is a blessing? Who said it were a curse? And what wine is this? It is, declares the Gulshan I Raz, the

> *"Wine, tasteless and odorless,*
> *Which washes away the writing on the tablet of Being."*

It is a drink which kindles a fire that burns forever and ever but does not consume the worshipper. It is the Sufi's idol. It leads captive all hearts.

The *Grape* is the whole sacred sexual congrex and is here correctly called a *veritable alchemist.* True Sex Magick *does not consume the worshipper;* it is regenerative.

Thus sang Fitzgerald:

60

The mighty Mahmud, Allah-breathing Lord,
That all the misbelieving and black Horde
Of Fears and Sorrows that infest the Soul
Scatters before him with his whirlwind Sword.

61

Why, be this Juice the growth of God, who dare
Blaspheme the twisted tendril as a Snare?
A Blessing, we should use it, should we not?
And if a Curse—why, then, Who set it there?

Thus spake Omar, the Sufi:

The Sufi urges you in the words of the Gulshan I Raz to "purge yourself from affirmations and negations," and give your mind wholly to the Cupbearer and His Wine. Remain not in the tangled wilds of wilfulness, but drink of Isa's cup. Buried in thyself thou canst not control the world or be the pivot of thy cycle. Give thyself up to His cup and thou shalt find thyself again in it. It is a giving, which is a getting. It is a sleep which is awakening! . . . The Sufi confesses with Shabistani:

"All my desire has been accomplished through Him,
Through Him I gained deliverance from infidel lust.
My heart was hid from knowledge of itself by a
*   hundred veils,*
By pride and vanity and self-conceit and illusion.
That fair idol entered my door at early morn
And wakened me from the sleep of negligence.
By His face the secret chamber of my soul was
*   illumined.*
Thereby I saw what I myself really am."

This is the regeneration to be attained when drinking *Isa's cup.*

Thus sang Fitzgerald:

65

The Revelations of Devout and Learn'd
Who rose before us, and as Prophets burn'd,
Are all but Stories, which, awoke from Sleep
They told their comrades and to Sleep return'd.

66

I sent my Soul through the Invisible,
Some letter of that After-life to spell:
And by and by my Soul return'd to me,
And answer'd "I Myself am Heav'n and Hell."

67

Heav'n but the Vision of fulfill'd Desire,
And Hell the Shadow from a Soul on fire
Cast on the Darkness into which Ourselves,
So late emerg'd from, shall so soon expire.

Thus spake Omar, the Sufi:

The Sufi disputes the sensual fact that

 "The Flower that once has blown forever dies."

The rose of yesterday is gone! True! Yet its aroma lingers upon my Soul. The maiden of last night is the matron of to-day. I ate the apple that yesterday held the life of futurity. All true! But is not yesterday a part of to-day? Is not that aroma the Breath of my Beloved? Are not the maiden and the matron the Motherhood of God? And the apple? Is that not fruitfulness? Where does it begin? Where does it end? Only the individual rose truly is! Only its aroma is aroma! Only my maiden is the mother! Only that apple is the apple! Individuality is nothing superadded nor anything subtracted! The pessimist does not say so! The Sufi says so! He stands for individuality and for immortality in the Beloved!

The spiritual attainment achieved through the sexual act does not die on the morrow; it lives long, that which approaches union with the *immortality in the Beloved.*

Thus sang Fitzgerald:

76

The Vine had struck a fibre: which about
If clings my Being—let the Dervish flout;
Of my Base metal may be filed a Key,
That shall unlock the Door he howls without.

77

And this I know: whether the one True Light
Kindle to Love, or Wrath—consume me quite,
One Flash of It within the Tavern caught
Better than in the Temple lost outright.

Thus spake Omar, the Sufi:

The Sufi Shabistani wrote over his door,

> *"Did ever one learn knowledge from the dead?*
> *Was ever lamp lighted from ashes?*
> *For this cause my mind is resolved on this,*
> *To gird my loins with the Magian girdle."*

And what is the Magian girdle? The vine! The mysteries of the orb and cycle are solved by its lines. It is "the line of beauty." It is warm with human passion and bright and heavenly light. It contains the creative principle and begets infinite love. Its sap turns us into artists. No oracular wisdom can vie with it. It is the revelation of revelations . . . Encircle yourself with the vine, "the knotted girdle," and you shall be equal to Khizr, "the green man," who drank of "the waters of life." You shall know the secret of Nadir and Zenith, of opposition and conjunction, and why the heavens are always in a whirl . . . You shall according to the Gulshan I Raz,

> *"Behold the world entirely comprised in yourself:*
> *You are the kernel of the world in the midst thereof.*
> *Know yourself that you are the world's soul."*

The above will become clear enough after only a few good practices of the sexual congrex.

Thus sang Fitzgerald:

98

Would but some winged Angel ere too late
Arrest the yet unfolded Roll of Fate,
And make the stern Recorder otherwise
Enregister, or quite obliterate!

99

Ah Love! could you and I with Him conspire
To grasp this sorry Scheme of Things entire,
Would not we shatter it to bits—and then
Re-mould it nearer to the Heart's desire!

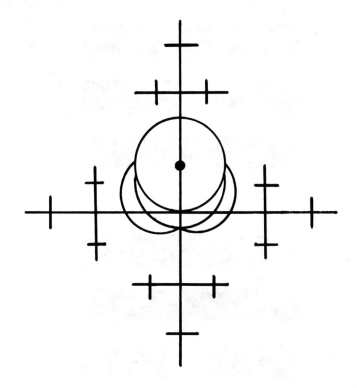

The Sigil of Baphomet

Under the Sigil of Baphomet is the partly secret assertion that it is the Sex Magick brought from the Arabian Sufis by certain Knights Templar Initiates. It contains both the sign of the Sun and Moon conjoined and the Baphomet Cross.

The Cauldron

This hexagram represents the best augury for high
Sex Magick. As the cooking cauldron transforms and
transmutes various substances to make them suitable
for human consumption, so the "cauldron," set over
the fire of magickal ecstasy and aspiration, transforms
the sexual impulse.

THE YI KING AND SEX MAGICK

The two outstanding translators of the original writings and the appendices on the Yi King—King Wan and his son—have stoutly maintained that the Yi contains no phallicism. Phallicism is a religious worship of the sex generative function and it is true that there is no evidence of this contained in the Yi writings.

But there is plenty of evidence that the ancient Chinese used the Yi King Oracle to determine the favorableness or unfavorableness of the next contemplated sexual union, and to determine the type of conditions that would prevail; however, both Wilhelm and Legge make no comment on this, if for no other reason than that both of them have clearly shown their subconscious sex inhibitions.

After receiving some pointers from an aged member of a very ancient and secret order devoted to the Yi King, known in this country as the Order of the Singing Fan, I have had no difficulty in decoding the meaning of each of the 64 Hexagrams of the Yi as pertaining to the propitiousness and nature of the next contemplated sexual union.

You will notice that the Yi Hexagrams are made up of various combinations of whole and broken lines. The whole line, called Yang, represents the masculine principle in Nature: the broken line, called Yin, represents the feminine principle.

The methods for casting the Yi King Oracle are quite different from the methods ordinarily used. There are three distinctive methods which can be used.

First Method. At the termination of the sexual union, but while the man and wife are still embracing, the wife concentrates to get the first mental picture of one of the eight trigrams. The husband does likewise. The wife's trigram is placed on the bottom of the hexagram; the husband's trigram on the top of the hexagram. To use this particular method it is necessary for both parties to become well enough acquainted with the appearance of the trigrams in order to visualize one of them clearly and to remember it long enough to draw it on paper. The resultant hexagram describes the nature of the next contemplated sexual congrex and whether it is favorable or not. If it is not favorable, wait at least two days before casting the hexagram as by the second method.

Second Method. This method can be done at any time previous to the next contemplated sexual union. The man and wife stand or sit facing each other, having a paper and pencil handy.

The hexagram is always built from the bottom upwards. The man announces the first line (bottom) saying male or female, whichever comes from impulse or feeling. This is written down. The woman likewise announces male or female which is also written down. This process is repeated until the six lines are completed to make the hexagram.

The day and time of the congrex must have been chosen before casting the hexagram. When you refer to the meaning of the numbered hexagram which has been erected, it may be found that it is unfavorable. You are therefore advised to select another hour and then erect another hexagram to determine the favorability. If this turns out to be unfavorable, you are advised to use method number three.

Third Method. This is the hour method. Most people will find this method to be the most practical and the most simple. The hour table gives the most favorable times according to the rulership of the various Yi King Hexagrams.

In this table is given the number of the hexagram which comes under the time indicated. A good procedure is to look over the meanings of the hexagrams and to choose the hexagram number that is most appealing for your purpose. Then simply look in the hour table to find out what time the chosen hexagram is in correspondence.

Clock time is exact only at the standard meridians. It is set for every 15 degrees of longitude beginning at Greenwich (0 degrees). Find out which meridian time is used in your location. To get the correct time, multiply the number of degrees you are, for example, east of your meridian, by the minutes. (The rate of 360 degrees in 24 hours equals 4 minutes for every degree.) Add this to your clock time. (5 degrees east of your meridian, 5 x 4 is 20 minutes; add 20 minutes to your clock time.) If you live west of your standard meridian follow the same procedure except subtract from your clock time for the correct time. Also, if daylight time is in force you must make a one hour adjustment.

There is something important to be said about the hexagrams 60, 61, 62, 63, and 64. These are good for only one thing: during Dianism these are very good for the husband in exercising the imagination in particular, and also for invoking the inspiration of being in rapport with the Divine Lover—the Holy Daemon, the Holy Guardian Angel. In this, the wife can be of very special aid and if she is, the special inspiration will reflect back to her.

YI KING HOUR TABLE

AM		HEX	AM		HEX
6:00 —	6:22½	1	9:00 —	9:22½	9
6:22½ —	6:45	2	9:22½ —	9:45	10
6:45 —	7:07½	3	9:45 —	10:07½	11
7:07½ —	7:30	4	10:07½ —	10:30	12
7:30 —	7:52½	5	10:30 —	10:52½	13
7:52½ —	8:15	6	10:52½ —	11:15	14
8:15 —	8:37½	7	11:15 —	11:37½	15
8:37½ —	9:00	8	11:37½ —	12 NOON	16

AM		HEX	AM		HEX
12:00 —	12:22½	48	3:00 —	3:22½	40
12:22½ —	12:45	47	3:22½ —	3:45	39
12:45 —	1:07½	46	3:45 —	4:07½	38
1:07½ —	1:30	45	4:07½ —	4:30	37
1:30 —	1:52½	44	4:30 —	4:52½	36
1:52½ —	2:15	43	4:52½ —	5:15	35
2:15 —	2:37½	42	5:15 —	5:37½	34
2:37½ —	3:00	41	5:37½ —	6:00	33

YI KING HOUR TABLE

PM		HEX		PM		HEX
12NOON —	12:22½	17		3:00 —	3:22½	25
12:22½ —	12:45	18		3:22½ —	3:45	26
12:45 —	1:07½	19		3:45 —	4:07½	27
1:07½ —	1:30	20		4:07½ —	4:30	28
1:30 —	1:52½	21		4:30 —	4:52½	29
1:52½ —	2:15	22		4:52½ —	5:15	30
2:15 —	2:37½	23		5:15 —	5:37½	31
2:37½ —	3:00	24		5:37½ —	6:00	32

PM		HEX		PM		HEX
6:00 —	6:22½	64		9:00 —	9:22½	56
6:22½ —	6:45	63		9:22½ —	9:45	55
6:45 —	7:07½	62		9:45 —	10:07½	54
7:07½ —	7:30	61		10:07½ —	10:30	53
7:30 —	7:52½	60		10:30 —	10:52½	52
7:52½ —	8:15	59		10:52½ —	11:15	51
8:15 —	8:37½	58		11:15 —	11:37½	50
8:37½ —	9:00	57		11:37½ —	12:00	49

The 64 Hexagrams

Upper Trigrams

Lower Trigrams

	KHIEN	AIR	SUN	EARTH	WATER	MOON	FIRE	KHWAN
	1	2	3	4	5	6	7	8
1	1	9	17	25	33	41	49	57
2	2	10	18	26	34	42	50	58
3	3	11	19	27	35	43	51	59
4	4	12	20	28	36	44	52	60
5	5	13	21	29	37	45	53	61
6	6	14	22	30	38	46	54	62
7	7	15	23	31	39	47	55	63
8	8	16	24	32	40	48	56	64

(1) Khien of Khien. There is not one line of Yin (the supporting and receptive female principle) and it is therefore not a good augury for intimate relations between man and wife. It is just "great starting energy". Good only for mutual aspiration in preparation for a future time.

(2) Air of Khien. The Wan text metaphorically describes this as, "A bold woman appears. Associate with her for only a short time; not good for long and no substantiality." Here is an auspice for physical sensuality but of no value in a substantial way; superficial and without inspiration.

(3) Sun of Khien. The lower trigram (Sun) means "brilliant realization" of a masculine type. Ordinarily this is not a good auspice for Sex Magick, but if the wife is capable of high aspiration and inspiration and has been so fortified, then it can be excellent.

(4) Earth of Khien. This is not essentially inspiring but is most excellent for bringing things to a consolidation, or fixed, material solidity. The husband can, however, with due diligence, give inspiration to his wife in a slow but determined and active way. Mostly recommended for only materialistic objectives.

(5) Water of Khien. Good for easy going, pleased satisfaction which comes easily and without restraint. Excellent for long-term Dianism if inspiration is welcomed.

(6) Moon of Khien. For a good auspice it is absolutely necessary that the wife invokes the strength, initiative, and support of her husband and does not try to press or exercise her own resources which are temporarily restricted. She must quell the tendency to be active, and instead be passive.

(7) Fire of Khien. There are two extremes—very favorable or very unfavorable. The fiery energy must be confined to make it feed the high imagination. One must not be engrossed in the physical ecstasy but utilize it to feed the fire of sincere and high purpose.

(8) Khwan of Khien. The Wan texts state in effect that "The female has come, the male has gone." If the wife's emotions and desires are not too demanding, but instead she is completely receptive, cooperative, and invoking the strong, correct Magick of the husband, then this can be one of the best. On the other hand, if she plays the part of wanting surfeit in sex from her husband, it is not a good augury for Sex Magick.

(9) Khien of Air. The Wan texts state, "If the wife exercises restraint, no matter how correct, she is in the position of the man

prosecuting his measures." In other words, this hexagram is not to be recommended for Sex Magick.

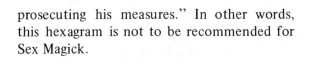

(10) Air of Air. Flighty and superficial, without substantiality on whatever plane. Not favorable for sexual congrex.

(11) Sun of Air. The Sun describes a condition where the woman is too forceful and dominant and the husband too pliable. In rare cases, the wife could be of great capabilities and well integrated, but it still advises you to wait.

(12) Earth of Air. Can be good only when there is a concentration of fixed purpose. Can be good in a practical way but there is also the liability of it being restrictive and constrictive. Must be a slow, gradual advance.

(13) Water of Air. There is not even any subconscious contention or dissatisfaction between the husband and wife. For the best results there should be no overemphasis of sexual pleasure or wild imagination; it is then one of the very best for Dianism and the received inspiration.

(14) Moon of Air. This is not a good augury for sexual congrex. It is well to by-pass these difficulties.

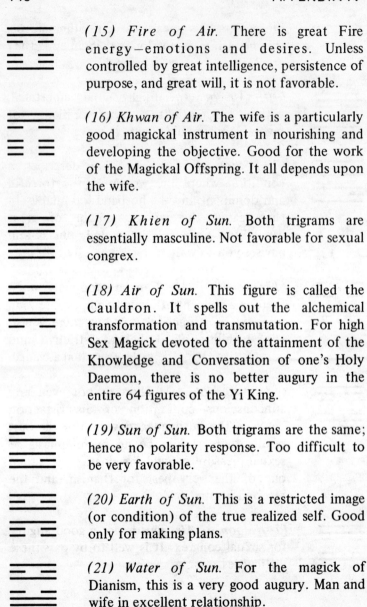

(15) Fire of Air. There is great Fire energy—emotions and desires. Unless controlled by great intelligence, persistence of purpose, and great will, it is not favorable.

(16) Khwan of Air. The wife is a particularly good magickal instrument in nourishing and developing the objective. Good for the work of the Magickal Offspring. It all depends upon the wife.

(17) Khien of Sun. Both trigrams are essentially masculine. Not favorable for sexual congrex.

(18) Air of Sun. This figure is called the Cauldron. It spells out the alchemical transformation and transmutation. For high Sex Magick devoted to the attainment of the Knowledge and Conversation of one's Holy Daemon, there is no better augury in the entire 64 figures of the Yi King.

(19) Sun of Sun. Both trigrams are the same; hence no polarity response. Too difficult to be very favorable.

(20) Earth of Sun. This is a restricted image (or condition) of the true realized self. Good only for making plans.

(21) Water of Sun. For the magick of Dianism, this is a very good augury. Man and wife in excellent relationship.

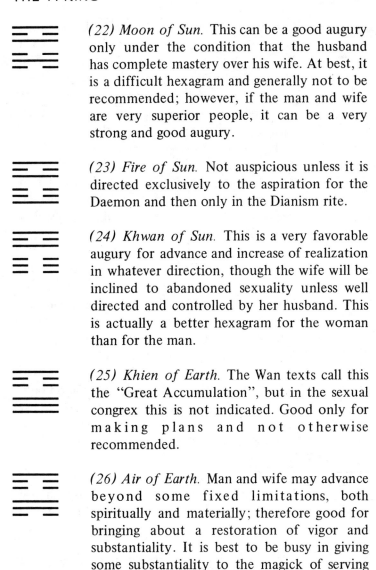

(22) Moon of Sun. This can be a good augury only under the condition that the husband has complete mastery over his wife. At best, it is a difficult hexagram and generally not to be recommended; however, if the man and wife are very superior people, it can be a very strong and good augury.

(23) Fire of Sun. Not auspicious unless it is directed exclusively to the aspiration for the Daemon and then only in the Dianism rite.

(24) Khwan of Sun. This is a very favorable augury for advance and increase of realization in whatever direction, though the wife will be inclined to abandoned sexuality unless well directed and controlled by her husband. This is actually a better hexagram for the woman than for the man.

(25) Khien of Earth. The Wan texts call this the "Great Accumulation", but in the sexual congrex this is not indicated. Good only for making plans and not otherwise recommended.

(26) Air of Earth. Man and wife may advance beyond some fixed limitations, both spiritually and materially; therefore good for bringing about a restoration of vigor and substantiality. It is best to be busy in giving some substantiality to the magick of serving the Divine Lover.

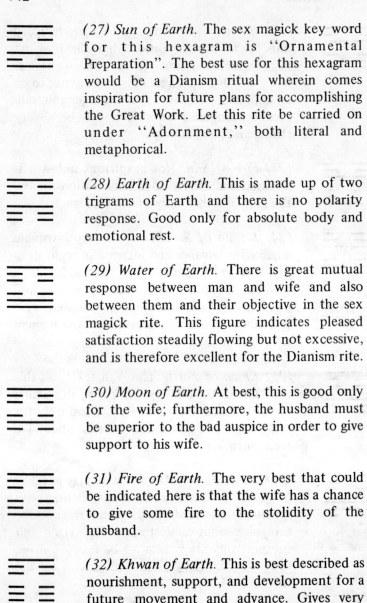

(27) Sun of Earth. The sex magick key word for this hexagram is "Ornamental Preparation". The best use for this hexagram would be a Dianism ritual wherein comes inspiration for future plans for accomplishing the Great Work. Let this rite be carried on under "Adornment," both literal and metaphorical.

(28) Earth of Earth. This is made up of two trigrams of Earth and there is no polarity response. Good only for absolute body and emotional rest.

(29) Water of Earth. There is great mutual response between man and wife and also between them and their objective in the sex magick rite. This figure indicates pleased satisfaction steadily flowing but not excessive, and is therefore excellent for the Dianism rite.

(30) Moon of Earth. At best, this is good only for the wife; furthermore, the husband must be superior to the bad auspice in order to give support to his wife.

(31) Fire of Earth. The very best that could be indicated here is that the wife has a chance to give some fire to the stolidity of the husband.

(32) Khwan of Earth. This is best described as nourishment, support, and development for a future movement and advance. Gives very

small promise for the actual present. Materialistic.

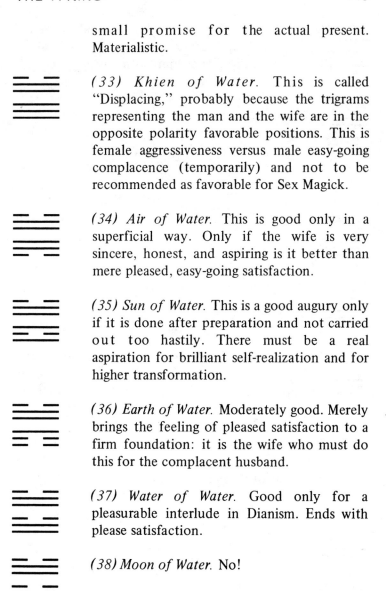

(33) Khien of Water. This is called "Displacing," probably because the trigrams representing the man and the wife are in the opposite polarity favorable positions. This is female aggressiveness versus male easy-going complacence (temporarily) and not to be recommended as favorable for Sex Magick.

(34) Air of Water. This is good only in a superficial way. Only if the wife is very sincere, honest, and aspiring is it better than mere pleased, easy-going satisfaction.

(35) Sun of Water. This is a good augury only if it is done after preparation and not carried out too hastily. There must be a real aspiration for brilliant self-realization and for higher transformation.

(36) Earth of Water. Moderately good. Merely brings the feeling of pleased satisfaction to a firm foundation: it is the wife who must do this for the complacent husband.

(37) Water of Water. Good only for a pleasurable interlude in Dianism. Ends with please satisfaction.

(38) Moon of Water. No!

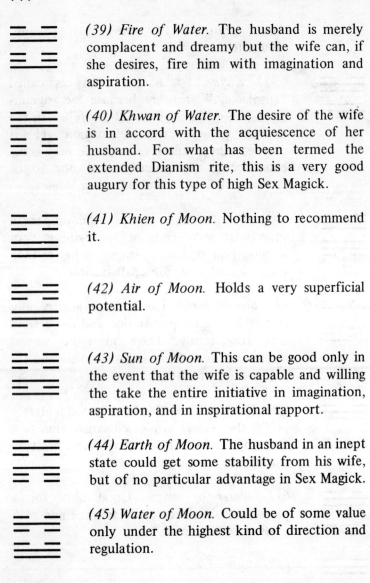

(39) Fire of Water. The husband is merely complacent and dreamy but the wife can, if she desires, fire him with imagination and aspiration.

(40) Khwan of Water. The desire of the wife is in accord with the acquiescence of her husband. For what has been termed the extended Dianism rite, this is a very good augury for this type of high Sex Magick.

(41) Khien of Moon. Nothing to recommend it.

(42) Air of Moon. Holds a very superficial potential.

(43) Sun of Moon. This can be good only in the event that the wife is capable and willing the take the entire initiative in imagination, aspiration, and in inspirational rapport.

(44) Earth of Moon. The husband in an inept state could get some stability from his wife, but of no particular advantage in Sex Magick.

(45) Water of Moon. Could be of some value only under the highest kind of direction and regulation.

(46) Moon of Moon. No.

(47) Fire of Moon. A rather distressing and disappointing struggle.

(48) Khwan of Moon. Only good if the husband excels exceedingly and then there would be great reward.

(49) Khien of Fire. No good promise.

(50) Air of Fire. Not good except for the most advanced.

(51) Sun of Fire. "First meet thy mate, then multiply thy force./Let not its accidents disturb thy course./United with sincerity, tis fortune's course." Under high aim and will, it is excellent for Sex Magick.

(52) Earth of Fire. This is recommended as a good augury for practice in harnessing emotional drives.

(53) Water of Fire. If the disparity between the lower trigram of Water which represents the desire for pleased satisfaction by the woman, and the upper trigram of Fire which

represents the compelling energy and force by the man, is not too great, then, and then only is it a good augury for Sex Magick. In other words, the woman is likely to desire too much satisfaction and sensuousness and the man too much driving, active force. Unless most of this is controlled it would not be a good augury.

(54) Moon of Fire. No.

(55) Fire of Fire. Mere misdirected Fire.

(56) Khwan of Fire. Great capacity and expansion of the awakened force and energy of the aspiration leading to great inspiration. Excellent for Sex Magick.

(57) Khien of Khwan. The great initiating energy lies with the wife for any good augury. Doubtful in most cases.

(58) Air of Khwan. Some superficial success: not generally good.

(59) Sun of Khwan. Advantageous to realize the difficulty of the position. The wife must be the husband and the husband must be the wife for success in Magick.

(60) Earth of Khwan. Good for preparation but that is all.

(61) Water of Khwan. Good for long-term Dianism.

(62) Moon of Khwan. Not good for long-term Dianism but good for the shorter term.

(63) Fire of Khwan. Not good for long-term Dianism but good for the shorter term.

(64) Khwan of Khwan. Good for reaching the quasi-trance state of long-term Dianism.

STAY IN TOUCH

On the following pages you will find listed, with their current prices, some of the books and tapes now available on related subjects. Your book dealer stocks most of these, and will stock new titles in the Llewellyn series as they become available. We urge your patronage.

However, to obtain our full catalog, to keep informed of new titles as they are released and to benefit from informative articles and helpful news, you are invited to write for our bi-monthly news magazine/catalog. A sample copy is free, and it will continue coming to you at no cost as long as you are an active mail customer. Or you may keep it coming for a full year with a donation of just $2.00 in U.S.A. ($7.00 for Canada & Mexico, $20.00 overseas, first class mail). Many bookstores also have *The Llewellyn New Times* available to their customers. Ask for it.

Stay in touch! In *The Llewellyn New Times'* pages you will find news and reviews of new books, tapes and services, announcements of meetings and seminars, articles helpful to our readers, news of authors, advertising of products and services, special money-making opportunities, and much more.

The Llewellyn New Times
P.O. Box 64383-Dept. 110, St. Paul, MN 55164-0383, U.S.A.

• • •

TO ORDER BOOKS AND TAPES

If your book dealer does not have the books and tapes described on the following pages readily available, you may order them direct from the publisher by sending full price in U.S. funds, plus $1.00 for handling and 50¢ each book or item for postage within the United States; outside USA surface mail add $1.50 per item postage and $1.00 per order for handling. Outside USA air mail add $7.00 per item postage and $1.00 per order for handling. MN residents add 6% sales tax.

FOR GROUP STUDY AND PURCHASE

Because there is a great deal of interest in group discussion and study of the subject matter of this book, we feel that we should encourage the adoption and use of this particular book by such groups by offering a special "quantity" price to group leaders or "agents".

Our Special Quantity Price for a minimum order of five copies of SEX MAGIC is $20.85 Cash-With-Order. This price includes postage and handling within the United States. Minnesota residents must add 6% sales tax. For additional quantities, please order in multiples of five. For Canadian and foreign orders, add postage and handling charges as above. Credit Card (VISA, MasterCard, American Express, Diners' Club) Orders are accepted. Charge Card Orders only may be phoned free ($15.00 minimum order) within the U.S.A. by dialing 1-800-THE MOON (in Canada call: 1-800-FOR-SELF). Customer Service calls dial 1-612-291-1970. Mail Orders to:

LLEWELLYN PUBLICATIONS
P.O. Box 64383-Dept. 110 / St. Paul, MN 55164-0383, U.S.A.